Transcendent Leadership and the Evolution of Consciousness

By

Lisa Aldon

To my fellow travelers in
Consciousness –
My love and appreciation

Lisa

505-980-0037

lisa@transcendentleadership.com

First Published by AuthorHouse 03/24/05

ISBN: 1-4208-3768-0 (e-book)
ISBN: 1-4208-3763-X (Paperback)

Library of Congress Control Number: 2005901854

This book is printed on acid free paper.

Printed in the United States of America
Bloomington, IN

INTRODUCTION TO THE BOOK

The following pages were written for my thesis to complete my Master's at the University of San Diego in Leadership Studies. It was originally published and cataloged at the University in 1998. At the time, we were "standing on the threshold of 21st century" but today, the view looks quite different. Humankind's search for meaning today is at the most critical of the new century. Do we annihilate each other due to hate and indifference and or oil?

Now, more than ever we need this quintessential understanding that we are all interconnected and evolving toward transcendence. I believe the leadership process truly can be the fulcrum of this understanding and awakening with each other and ourselves.

Whether it is the child putting up flyers of peace, emails being forwarded all over the world for petitions for peace, or the masses demonstrating for worldwide peace, this is the power of leadership within each of us.

Let's begin it now...

ACKNOWLEDGEMENTS

The author would like to acknowledge my father, Earl Aldon, my sister, Lauryann Aldon, and my three friends who believed in me enough to recommend me for acceptance into the Leadership Studies program; Ed Zell, Steve Gates and John Dentico. Thanks guys, what a ride!

To Steve Turnbull my manager at Solar Turbines, for the support, the time and funding (from Solar).

And to all of my friends for there continued support, encouragement, patience, and love through this process.

But, I would like to especially acknowledge John Dentico for introducing me to this wonderful program which allowed me to continue my passion of the study of leadership. And for all his help, empathy, sympathy, encouragement, great wine and especially his laughter and humor to keep us sane during this process. Thanks John.

Front artwork design by Edward Buckley.

DEDICATION

I would like to dedicate this thesis to my father, my mother and my friend Sam Ropelato.

My father for his never ending support of my growth, development, further education and love. Thanks Dad.

For my mother, whose life was too short on this planet, which propelled me in my search. "In searching for my mother's garden, I found my own".

And for my friend Sam, who, during the writing of this thesis left this planet to rid himself of his pain. He taught me the quintessential lesson of compassion, for without compassion, we have lost God. Sammy, this one's for you, I hope you found peace…

TABLE OF CONTENTS

LIST OF FIGURES

LIST OF TABLES

CHAPTER ONE

Humankind stands at the threshold of the 21st century as members of a society whose complex issues seem overwhelming and endless. Just beyond the threshold, we see an exciting future of incredible turbulence and change, a place where, despite the maelstrom, a significant number of people will continue to pursue happiness and meaning. Why is humankind's search for meaning rising to the surface now, more than ever? As Peter Drucker has stated, "This is far more than a social change, it is a change in the human condition" (Drucker, 1994). Looking through the door of tomorrow, we recognize two very different paths, an abyss in between, and attempts to bridge the gap between the two roads.

Historically, the split between the two paths began around 1800, during the European Age of Enlightenment. The path to the right, was traveled by those who broke with tradition and chose to seek something more than what German sociologist philosopher Jurgen Habermas called "the blind veneration of classical antiquity" (Habermas quoted in Smart, 1990, p.14), where science replaced God at the alter of conscious thought and action. People's yearning to

1

escape religious oppression grew from the cruelties inflicted on men and women in the name of God as the movement toward individual rights and freedoms erupted. The credo of the enlightened was that true liberation and freedom were found in "real" gains on earth: progress in actual social conditions (economic and material worth) and political freedoms. But this path on the right was narrow and shallow, and left many people searching for something greater.

The path to the left is the continuation of a path where walked conservatives who remained bound to classical dogma. They were wedded more to a traditional view in which men and women depended on communal standards and values, including predominant formal religious beliefs. The ultimate concern of these people their relationship to the "right" God. The left-hand path was a paradoxical one where righteousness and justice in the name of God resulted in travesties of righteousness and justice in the name of God. Many travelers along this path experienced fear, anger, and ultimate disconnection and fragmentation from the rest of humanity and the true meaning of God. How could the symbol of unity and happiness,

God, create alienation and frustration? Transpersonal psychologist and author Ken Wilber (1997) summarized the answer to this question in the following:

> The most pressing political issue of the day, both in America and abroad, is a way to integrate the tradition of liberalism with a genuine spirituality. Never in history have these two strands of human striving been woven together in any sort of acceptable fashion. In fact, modern liberalism (and the general movement of the European Enlightenment) came into being in large measure precisely as a force against traditional religion. (p. xiii)

An attempt to integrate these two paths can be found in a "spiritual humanistic" (Wilber, 1997) roadway that sets the rights of the individual in deeper spiritual contexts, a path that does not deny those rights but grounds them in the essence and character of our humanness to go beyond one's self in the unity and spirit of community. Along this roadway lie bricks for building this integrated path: values of trust, respect, love, integrity, and the spirit of community. The full spectrum of consciousness, the continued development of humankind, acts as the mortar, providing the context that binds the bricks together in a continuum for our own evolution, the continued development of humankind. In addition, a surveyed line, looking very much like an umbilical cord, forming a web of interconnection and interdependence, stretches out past the horizon, originating from the first life on the planet. While we cannot see its end, we understand, as the classical adage says, that the journey of a thousand miles begins with one step.

Gathered at the threshold, we look in each other's eyes and realize we are connected and are truly on the same path. Psychologist and concentration camp survivor Victor Frankl (1969) wrote that "human existence is not authentic unless it is lived in terms of self-transcendence . . . for it is a characteristic constituent of human existence that it transcends itself, that it reaches out for something other than itself" (p. 55). We are on the same path precisely because we are transcendent, because we all are reaching out for something beyond ourselves.

Is there a process to provide the opportunity for people to connect in the essence of spiritual humanism to undertake great and difficult tasks, provide holistic contexts from which we can create our future together, and cause us to take charge of our own evolution as we transcend? Could this be the true nature of leadership?

This purpose of this study will suggest that leadership theories are inadequate unless they include transcendence as an essential element influencing human behavior. This author believes that if transcendence is included in leadership theories, an ebb and flow relationship will exist, providing opportunities where introspection and reflection of one's role can cause individual transcendence to a higher level of consciousness, while at the same time causing transforming change in the individual and the organization. As James MacGregor Burns (1978) wrote, transforming leadership happens when "people raise one another to higher levels of motivation and morality" (p. 20).

This author also believes that the leadership relationship offers a great opportunity to conflate "traditional liberalism with genuine spirituality" (Wilber, 1997), to not only raise one another to higher levels of motivation, morality, and consciousness, but to co-create the future in the essence of "spiritual humanism" (p. xvi). This study will examine theories of the evolution of consciousness as the context for understanding transcendence. Utilizing the elements of transcendence and consciousness as a foundation, these concepts could help further not only the study, but the practice of leadership as well.

The research strategy used in this exploratory study is based on an extensive review of literature on leadership theories as embodied from a science and technology perspective (the path on the right), overarching religious themes (the path on the left), humanistic sciences (the abyss between the paths), spiritual leadership (an attempt to bridge the abyss), and the evolution of consciousness theories (the model to span the abyss and converge the paths). In summary, this author will urge the development of a leadership model that includes transcendence as an essential basic element. It is envisioned that such a model that is grounded in spiritual humanism can bring people to higher levels of consciousness.

Background

Vaclav Havel, playwright, dissident, prisoner, and former president of Czechoslovakia, speaking about the Czech republic's people, felt they were living in the middle of the first "atheistic civilization," the effect of which was an "arrogant anthropocentrism," or self-centeredness. He believed they had lost touch with any understanding that there is something greater than what we perceive as reality, or "transcendent reality." The irony, he states, was that at the moment human beings placed themselves at the summit of meaning in the world and took themselves to be the measure of everything, their economies would began to take the measure of them (In *Spirit at Work,* edited by Jay Conger, 1994, p. 48). Havel concluded that the net effect of a critical mass yielding to this temptation was a deeply demoralized people (p. 47, 48). Although Havel was talking about the Czech republic, it seems more than one nation lives in a demoralized society, divided and fragmented by traditional liberalism and conservative religion (Wilber 1997).

Lisa Aldon

The path on the right

The industrial era has been depicted as a well-oiled machine: rational, precise, and based on the Newtonian science of mechanistic thought. Command and control defined leadership for this era; intimidation, fear, superiority. The process belonged to "the man" at the top of a hierarchical organization. Organizations of all types followed this model, in which people were treated as parts and indeed cogs in the wheel of progress.

By the end of World War II, the shift from physical labor to human knowledge as the prime mover in the United States had begun and the transformation from an industrial to a postindustrial perspective was picking up speed. Surprisingly as early as 1955, the number of service workers surpassed the number of manufacturing workers (Toffler and Toffler, 1995). Since then the ratio has been widening steadily, "by 1970 the white-collar workers outnumbered the blue-collar by more than five to four" (Bell, 1973. p. 17). Yet while the shift to the postindustrial began, leadership remained primarily hierarchical, with the belief that a good leader was a good manager whose job was to assure strict compliance with the rules and regulations of the organization, scientifically measure the outputs and worth of each individual's contribution while maintaining strict control over those who were subordinate to him.

As William O'Brien (1998) stated "that applying scientific attitudes to human behavior had backfired, because reductionistic perspectives stifled creativity, ingenuity, trust, perseverance, and other gifts of human nature that directly fuel business performance and personal happiness. . . Human beings are much more than numbers and machines, and have far more dimensions to them besides just the rational" (O'Brien, 1998, p.2). Peter Senge went a step further:

> Even though our political and institutional leadership is losing respect and credibility, and core societal crises fester, we are gaining a greater understanding of how the universe works. An historic shift in the Western-scientific-materialistic world view is occurring. Perhaps the two are connected. Perhaps our institutions and leadership are, by and large, grounded in a way of thinking about the world that is

increasingly obsolete and counterproductive. Perhaps
that is why they are falling apart. (Introduction in
Jaworski, 1997, p.3)

Our society is demoralized, perhaps because we've lost touch with our spiritual selves, relying on science, technology, and intellect to solve the problems of our souls, forgetting there is something greater than ourselves, and placing ourselves at the "summit of meaning." Havel asserted that the core perversity is the refusal of individuals to take responsibility for personal and organizational renewal. Responsibility is avoided. "If people were in touch with their own consciences, they would freely invest themselves in creating structures and organizations to meet human needs" (In Conger, Ed., 1994, p.54).

Lee Bolman and Terry Deal (1995), pioneers in organizational development, summarized viewpoints similar to Havel's:

Technology continues to march ahead, yet chronic
social and economic problems get worse. Communities
suffer from levels of crime, chemical dependence, and

alienation unprecedented in a civilized society. Families and children are in more trouble than at any time in recent memory. Many schools are ruled by gangs and ripped by violence. Children murder children. Has our contemporary emphasis on reason and progress put us on a one-way street to personal anguish and social disarray? (p. 4, 5)

As we move into the postindustrial era of complex change, a population rich in diversity and information available to everyone, will industrial leadership concepts suffice? Peter Senge says no: "The sixteenth-century Newtonian mechanical view of the universe, which still guides our thinking, has become increasingly dysfunctional in these times of interdependence and change." (Senge in Jaworski, 1997, p.9).

In his doctoral dissertation for the School of Education at the University of San Diego, Richard Henrickson (1989) presented an enormous and thorough review of the literature of leadership, noting that although there are more than 5,000 studies on leadership we are no closer to defining or understanding what leadership is and is not.

Henrickson concluded that there is no universal ethic in leadership because the disciplines of philosophy, anthropology, psychology, sociology, and biology have not formulated basic categories of a universal ethic. However, Henrickson does say that there is no doubt that leadership has an intrinsic ethical dimension.

Many leadership scholars and popular leadership/management writers have stated in one way or another that the process of acquiring self-knowledge is a fundamental route to effective leadership. Proponents of this theory include James MacGregor Burns, Peter Block, Lee Bolman and Terry Deal, and Warren Bennis, to name a few. James Kouzes and Barry Posner (1996), in their book *The Leadership Challenge,* wrote, "Ultimately, leadership development is a process of self-development . . . The quest for leadership is first an inner quest to discover who you are" (p. 336).

Even though these leadership scholars and authors recognize self-knowledge as fundamental, they do not explore what leadership might look like beyond self-knowledge. Ronald A. Heifetz (1994), psychiatrist and director of leadership education at Harvard's Kennedy School of Government, in his book, *Leadership Without*

Easy Answers, stressed the idea that we need to stop looking to others for the answers, but rather, we need to look within ourselves .

The path on the left

The sacred texts and traditions of world religions reveal similarities in what Herb Barker in his doctoral dissertation labeled a "global ethic." Barker's dissertation, along with Houston Smith's (1991) acclaimed work, *Illustrated World's Religions: A Guide to Our Wisdom Traditions,* provides a comprehensive, intellectual, and spiritual journey of encounters with our eastern and western wisdom traditions. These sources, along with others, will provide overviews of human spirituality, framed in religion and sacred tradition.

The paths conflate

In his groundbreaking books on consciousness, Ken Wilber offers a comprehensive, integrated, and visionary theory. His integral vision considers all aspects of humanity, from philosophy, art, science, psychology, and neurology to mysticism, religion, and spirituality. His model looks at the self's transcending stages of consciousness from physical or sensor stage to the "unity conscious" stage. These stages show a path beyond ego to a transcending connection with something greater than ourselves. Wilber's "master template" honors and connects with the essence of the world's wisdom traditions, while simultaneously blending with modern knowledge (1995, p.38). This integrated view, or integral model of self, offers not only the span of understanding in terms of the amount of the number of stages of consciousness, but the depth and breadth of research and information within each stage, presented in his work. This model will show that we are indeed not only capable of transcendence, but it is our nature, as Havel and Frankl stated.

The path for the 21ˢᵗ Century

This research may give us a picture of the critical interdependence of consciousness and the leadership relationship. In the end, this study could reveal Burns (1978), Heifetz (1994), Bennis (1997), and others' acknowledgments that values, ethics, and morality are not only integral to the phenomenon of leadership but are strengthened and better integrated within a model of consciousness, with transcendence.

Bolman and Deal (1995) wrote: "Heart, hope, and faith, rooted in soul and spirit, are necessary for today's managers to become tomorrow's leaders, for today's sterile bureaucracies to become tomorrow's communities of meaning, and for our society to rediscover its ethical and spiritual center" (p. 12). Peter Senge feels we have exhausted our current way of thinking, and leadership can be a catalyst:

> The critical shifts required to guarantee a healthy world for our children and our children's children will not be achieved by doing more of the same. "The world we have created is a product of our way of thinking," said Einstein. Nothing will change in the future without fundamentally new ways of thinking. This is the real work of leadership. (Introduction in Jaworski, 1997, p.9)

In order to center our discussions, the following definitions support the remainder of the study.

Definitions

Leadership - For the purpose of this thesis, leadership as a process, utilizing the postindustrial definition will be used unless otherwise stated, In discussing the task of defining leadership, Heifetz (1994) writes: It seems to me that scholars might usefully consider that leadership is less an "is" than a "should be," and that our arguments might center not around who has most accurately described objective reality (or perhaps prevailing cultural assumptions) but around what image we can usefully offer to people who in part shape their self-images by our conceptions (p. 286)..

Post-industrial leadership - One definition is "an influence relationship among leaders and collaborators who intend real changes that reflect their mutual purpose" (Rost, 1991, p.102).

Body – the emotional body, sex, hunger, vital life forces (as studied by biology).

Mind – rational, reasoning, linguistic and imaginative mind (as studied by psychology).

Soul – the higher or subtle mind, the archetypal mind, the intuitive mind, and the essence or the indestructibleness of our own being (as studied by theology).

Spirit – the transcendental summit of our being, our Godhead. Both the highest goal of development and evolution and the ground of the entire sequence (as studied by contemplative mysticism). Another definition of spirit is "that which is traditionally believed to be the vital principle or animating force within living beings; that which constitutes one's unseen intangible being; the real sense or significance of something" (Scott, 1994, p. 64).

Spiritual - of, pertaining to, or consisting of spirit.

Hierarchy – a ranking of orders of events according to their holistic capacity. When explaining the evolution of consciousness, there are stages within the model. This would imply a hierarchy. Hierarchy in this sense does not indicate "higher" or "better," but rather a progression all-inclusive and all-embracing of the stages before it. In addition, this progression is a "higher"-archy, because it does not occur in the reverse. "All developmental and evolutionary sequences that we are aware of proceed in large measure by hierarchization, or by orders of increasing holism, molecules to cells to organs to organ systems to organisms to societies of organisms, for example" (Wilber, 1997, p.41). Another way of describing these stages is in terms of "holarchy."

Holarchy - A series of concentric circles of increasing inclusiveness. What is whole at one stage becomes merely a part of a larger whole at the next stage. Each stage unfolds and then enfolds its predecessors in a nested fashion.

Transcendence - To rise above our own perception of reality; to exist above and independent of, exceeding usual limits such as when we are able to extend our vision and feelings beyond the ordinary to discern an extraordinary, godly presence in our lives and universe. The process of becoming Spirit.

CHAPTER TWO

Review of Literature

Introduction

Following the analogy of the two paths presented in Chapter One, traditional liberalism and religion/spirituality will be reviewed from a historical perspective, beginning with the European Age of Enlightenment and continuing into the industrial and post-industrial eras. The abyss will be discussed and the bridges (attempts to merge or "bridge" the abyss) will be reviewed by looking at humanistic science literature. The convergence of the paths will be demonstrated through the development of an evolution of consciousness model.

Since many books and articles have been written on these subjects, only generally accepted wisdom or paramount themes and core concepts will be reviewed and presented for each topic.

SECTION 1

The Path on the Right: A Brief History of Society, Organizations, and Leadership (Modern to Postmodern)

Modern

Society - Individualism.

Agriculture provided the first demonstration of humanity's increasing control over his environment. Expansion of knowledge in metallurgy, engineering instruments, and clocks began the industrial era (Roberts, 1993). The diffusion of technical knowledge accelerated social change. "Industrialization would hardly have been possible without greater literacy and a part of what has been called a 'scientific revolution' in the seventeenth century must be attributed to the simple cumulative effect of more rapidly and widely circulated information" (p. 539).

Modern individualism emerged from the struggle against monarchical and aristocratic authority that seemed arbitrary and oppressive to citizens who were prepared to assert the right to govern themselves. Classical political philosophy and biblical religion inspired a notion of government based on the voluntary participation of individuals, (Bellah, Madsen, Sullivan, Swidler, and Tipton, 1985). John Locke published the biological individual perspective in a "state of nature" that "derived a social order from the actions of such individual, first in relation to nature and then in relation to one another . . . the individual is prior to society, which comes into existence only through the voluntary contract of individual trying to maximize their own self-interest" (p. 143). Machiavelli added to this with his influential book, *The Prince*. He combined individualism and power with statements such as "He who is the cause of another's greatness is himself undone, since he must work either by address or force, each of which excites distrust in the person's raised to power" (1532/1986, p. 16), and "On entering a new Princedom, judges it necessary to rid himself of enemies, to conciliate friends, to prevail by force or fraud, to make himself feared yet not hated by his subjects, respected and obeyed . . ." (p. 29).

Modern individualism has driven individual rights and individual autonomy into confrontation with those aspects of biblical and conservative thought that have caused unequal rights and obligation to emerge. To that end, the emphasis of the liberal democratic perspective, which exalts one's individual rights, has created a perception of a nation of separate and distinct individuals. However, as Casssel (1996) stated,

> The basic principle on which democracy rests is "the interdependence of independent individuals," and interdependence is always global in nature; as opposed to including only groups of local origin. Because of the global nature of the interdependence, democracy always includes cosmic consciousness, which is too often neglected in both theory and practice. (p.1)

DeTocqueville warned that "individualism also weakens the very meanings that give content and substance to the ideal of individual dignity" (Bellah, et al., 1985, p. 144). Modern individualism seems to be producing a way of life that is neither individually nor socially viable. Tocqueville also pointed out one of the ambiguities in individualism that was strangely compatible with conformism:

When the inhabitant of a democratic country compares himself individually with all those about him, he feels with pride that he is the equal of any one of them; but when he comes to survey the totality of his fellows and to place himself in contrast with so huge a body, he is instantly overwhelmed by the sense of his own insignificance and weakness. The equality that renders him independent of each of his fellow citizens, taken severally, exposes him alone and unprotected to the influence of the greater number. (1840/1990, p. 10)

This ambiguity and ambivalence derives from underlying cultural and social contradictions. We insist on finding our true selves, independent of any cultural or social influence, and being responsible to that self alone. Yet we spend much of our time in bureaucratic organizations and corporations, manipulating and being manipulated by others. Alasdair MacInyre coined the phrase "bureaucratic individualism" to describe the phenomenon:

Ambiguities and contradictions of individualism are frighteningly revealed, as freedom to make private decisions is bought at the cost of turning over most public decisions to bureaucratic managers and experts. A bureaucratic individualism in which the consent of the governed, the first demand of modern enlightened individualism, has been abandoned in all but form, illustrates the tendency of individualism to destroy its own conditions. (Bellah, et al., 1985, p. 150)

Organizations

Simply stated, organizing is concerned with bringing together a group of people to achieve some purpose. The most prevalent models for organizations were mechanistic in structure and focus. The earliest origins of the mechanistic model were taken from the military and can be accredited to Frederick the Great, who ruled Prussia from 1740 to 1786. "To ensure his military machine operated on command, Frederick fostered the principle that men must be taught to fear their officers more than the enemy" (Morgan, 1986, p. 24).

Adam Smith's division of labor, Charles Babbage's scientific approach to organizations, Henri Fayol's administrative theory of management, and Max Weber's observation of the parallels between the mechanization of industry and the proliferation of bureaucratic forms of organization all contributed to the mechanical mode of organizations that operated like machines—routine, efficient, reliable, and predictable. Fredrick Taylor's scientific management principles also underscored the need and desire for efficiency in the workplace. The mechanistic approach to organizations works well only under conditions where machines work well: where the task is straightforward, the environment is stable, and the human "machine" is compliant and behave as it has been designed to. But Morgan (1986) asserts that "in understanding organizations as a rational, technical process, mechanical imagery tends to under play the human aspects of organization" (p.34) and aids in the "assault of rationalism upon the human spirit" (p. 20).

Sociologist Max Weber saw that the bureaucratic approach had the potential "to routinize and mechanize almost every aspect of human life, eroding the human spirit and capacity for spontaneous action. He also recognized it could have political consequences in undermining the potential for democratic forms of organizations" (Morgan, 1986, p. 25). Bureaucracy required that one person, the leader who sat at the top of the pyramid, "performed" leadership. And in times when information was limited, when business was performed at a local rather than a global level, and when change did not occur as fast as it does today, this model seemed to work.

Leadership Studies

Jeffery Mello (1998), a professor at Golden Gate University, recently wrote an article titled "Reframing Leadership Pedagogy through Model and Theory Building." He believes that a comprehensive study of leadership and leadership effectiveness can be found in Greek and Latin classics, the Old and the New Testaments, and writings of ancient Chinese philosophers. "Given such a far-reaching history, it would seem that there should be some clear and consistent definition of leadership. However, despite the fact that numerous researchers and theorists have described and explained the same phenomenon, there has been no consistent definition of leadership" (p. 1). Burns (1978) seems to agree with him: "If we know too much about our leaders, we know far too little about leadership" (p.1). In addition, the fallacy of remaining open to every suggestion of what leadership might be not only continues to allow each individual researcher his or her own definition of leadership, but also fails to enable us to chart a clear course into the future.

Thus it appears that it is more imperative to identify the critical ingredients in affective leadership rather than a definition that only serves to give a fake impression of understanding. Leadership has been defined in terms of individual personality traits, leader behaviors, responses to leader behaviors, role relationships, follower perceptions, task goals, organizational culture, interaction patterns, and nature of work processes. Mello (1998) summarized the history of leadership, concentrating on the dominant approaches in the 20th century. He described four dominant paradigms where each approach has been an extension of and response to the criticisms of the previously dominant paradigm. "Individually each approach lends some valuable insights toward leadership but fails to provide a universal 'perfect theory' to aid in our understanding" (p.2). In brief, the four movements were (1) traits or characteristics of leaders (2) observable behaviors of leaders, (3) situational analyses of leadership, and (4) "outstanding leadership theory" [author's quotes]. All of these theories concentrate on the leader; the first three focus on individual and small group aspects while the last moves toward an examination of how leaders impact structure, culture, and performance within entire organizations. This is where Mello concluded his leadership theory movement. He failed to include what has been termed the transformational movement, which includes authors and scholars such as James MacGregor Burns, critical theorist William Foster, and Joseph Rost. The transformational or transforming movement identifies leadership as the actions of the collective dynamic, where relationships and the process of accomplishing a common purpose are key.

In contrast, seventy years ago Mary Parker Follet, a "pioneer, a swashbuckling advance soul of management thinking," as Warren Bennis called her, wrote and lectured on her ideas of organizations, leadership, power, and society. She was interested in the individual in society and how one could attain personal fulfillment while striving at the same time to create the well-ordered and just society. "The answer, she concluded, lay in democratic governance . . ."(Graham, 1995, p.15). Follett urged management of the time to reconsider the power-over model because it is reductionist and self-defeating. Her model was "power-with," an interactive influence going on all the time, jointly developing, and unifying (1995). Yet industrial grounded leaders turned a blind eye toward the meaning and acceptance of her perspective.

As society moves into great change on a global scale, answers from a humanistic perspective appears to better support this environment.

> Here again, the root problem is the folly of trying to operate with Lockean principles in an un-Lockean world. In conditions of general instability, it is dangerous for economic actors, either individual or corporate, to rely nearly exclusively on the short-term strategic logic of narrowly interpreted self-interest".
> (Bellah, et.al., 1991, pp. 101–102)

Rost (1992), professor emeritus of the University of San Diego, stated in his article entitled "Leadership and Shared Governance" that,

> . . . there is the view that what we are doing will not be acceptable in the next century even if we do what we are doing better. . . . Our present structures, policies, strategies, and practices are no longer adequate to solve our present problems. (p. 4)

This is a clear sign, Rost says, that the operating paradigm is on its way out and a shift is in process.

Using Socrates's analogy of the cave in Plato's Republic, Morgan (1986) asserts that people can actually become imprisoned or confined by the images, ideas, thoughts, and actions to which they have become bound (p. 15). As society emerges from the cave and undergoes a paradigmatic change of great enormity, the mechanistic view of organization and the lone autocratic leader are being discarded by our humanistic search for a greater sense of meaning in our lives.

Postmodern - Mass Communication, Global Economy, Rapid Change Society

The industrial era has evolved into a post-industrial era based on knowledge. As Peter Drucker states, this is the first society in which not everybody does the same work, as was the case when the majority were farmers, or machine operators. "This is far more than a social change. It is a change in the human condition" (1994, p. 64). In a post-industrial society, the disjunction of culture and social structure is bound to widen. Daniel Bell, in his watershed book *The Coming of the Post-Industrial Society*, writes:

> Material goods provide only transient satisfaction or an invidious superiority over those with less. Yet one of the deepest human impulses is to sanctify their institutions and beliefs in order to find a meaningful purpose in their lives and to deny the meaninglessness of death. . . . The lack of a rooted moral belief system

is the cultural contradiction of the society, the deepest challenge to its survival (p. 480).

In this regard, the search for personal happiness and meaning is experienced in many places. For example, the best-selling books for the last 15 to 20 years have been about people's search for meaning and spirituality. *The Road Less Traveled,* M. Scott Peck's book about psychological and spiritual development, has remained on the best-seller list for more than 11 years. Peck continued his journey in self-awareness in *The Different Drum.* The experience of community would create a new "connectedness" and wholeness. He wrote:

> Because of a multiplicity of factors—most particularly instant, mass communication . . . and the availability of psychotherapy that leads us to question the programs, cultural and otherwise, within which we were raised—the number of people entering the mystical stage of development and transcending ordinary culture seems to have increased a thousandfold in the course of a mere generation or two.

. . Still, one wonders if the explosion in their numbers might represent a giant leap forward in the evolution of the human race, a lead toward not only mystical but global consciousness and world community. (1987, pp. 205, 206)

In effect, the discourse surrounding a renewed sense of human connectedness is reflective of not only our personal lives but our organizational lives as well. As organizations are being transformed, so too leadership is undergoing substantial change.

This Newtonian perspective where man is seen as the top of the hierarchy of life on the planet, commander of his environment, and the summit of meaning is no longer adequate to sustain the effort required to deal with ever increasing complex dilemmas. Leadership in the 21st century must be relevant to a world filled with complexity, chaos, and continuing change.

Fritjof Capra (1990), in *Belonging to the Universe*, calls the new paradigm an "ecological paradigm" where systems theory is the scientific formulation of the ecological worldview (p. 72). Systems theory and the new paradigm are the shift from the parts to the whole.

The old paradigm stated that, in any complex system, the dynamics of the whole could be understood from the properties of the parts. In the new paradigm, the relationship between the parts and the whole is reversed, says Capra (p.83). "The properties of the parts can be understood only from the dynamics of the whole. Ultimately, there are no parts at all. What we call a part is merely a pattern in an inseparable web of relationships" (p. 83). This view is ultimately inclusive of all systems: biological, environmental, organizational, societal, and democratic, within the largest living "system," Gaia, the Earth.

Ronald Heifetz (1994) says we cannot continue to look to leaders for the answers; issues are complex, interconnected and defy simple solutions:

> In a crisis we tend to look for the wrong kind of leadership. We call for someone with answers, decision, strength, and a map of the future, someone who knows where we ought to be going—in short, someone who can make hard problems simple. But problems like the Los Angeles riots are not simple. . . .

We have many such problems: uncompetitive industry, drug abuse, poverty, poor public education . . . Making progress on these problems demands not just someone who provides answers from on high but changes in our attitudes, behavior, and values. To meet challenges such as these, we need a different idea of leadership and a new social contract that promote our adaptive capacities, rather than inappropriate expectations of authority. (p. 2)

As the new paradigm of systems thinking filters into society, so too it filters into organizations. The movement from parts to the whole, relationships, and the process of becoming seems to be the dominating themes. What concept best describes this phenomenon? What concept captures this process of becoming as it occurs at an individual level of analysis, at an organizational level, and indeed, at a global level?

Lisa Aldon

Organizations

·

In *The Ecology of Commerce*, Paul Hawken (1993) stated that "corporations, because they are the dominant institution on the planet, must squarely address the social and environmental problems that afflict humankind" (p.13). He went on to say that in order to create an enduring society, we will need a system of commerce and production where each and every act is "inherently sustainable and restorative" (p. 14). Business will need to integrate economic, biologic, and human systems to create a sustainable method of commerce. We know that every natural system on the planet is disintegrating. The land, water, air, and sea have been functionally transformed from life-supporting systems into repositories for waste. Given current corporate practices, not one wildlife reserve, wilderness, or indigenous culture will survive the global market economy. "Our human destiny is inextricably linked to the actions of all other living things. Respecting this principle is the fundamental challenge in changing the nature of business" (p.16). Hawken suggests we have a systemic problem that involves both people and commerce. This interrelationship among all living things suggests the complexity of continuum improvement, of becoming better that before.

The viable solutions to present day problems are those that do not create other problems in the future. The only solutions that are acceptable are sustainable solutions. Lester Brown of the Worldwatch Institute says, "A sustainable society is one that satisfies its needs without diminishing the prospects of future generations" (in Capra, 1993, p. 166).

With the understanding of interconnectedness and the important role organizations are providing, it seems that the linchpin of progress is in an organizations ability to harness, interpret and implement the collective insights of its membership. These implemented collective insights are a kind of "social capital".

Robert Putnam's (1995) definition of "social capital" is "features of social organization such as networks, norms and social trust that facilitate coordination and cooperation for mutual benefit" (p.4). He goes stresses, "researchers in such fields as education, urban poverty, unemployment, the control of crime and drug abuse, and even health have discovered that successful outcomes are more likely in civically engaged communities" (p.3).

Peter Senge also agrees with the criticality of incorporating systems thinking in "the learning organization." In order for organizations to realize their highest aspirations, five dimensions— systems thinking, personal mastery, mental models, building shared vision, and team learning must be operating. Senge states that when people are part of a great team, when they are in a "deeper learning," they talk about "being part of something larger than themselves, of being connected, of being generative" (1990, p. 13). He calls this "metanoia," meaning a fundamental shift of mind, or more literally, transcendence of mind. He also believes, as Hawken does, that organizations have the greatest opportunity to "shift the minds" of society, thereby contributing to progress and a better world.

Building learning organization involves developing people who learn to see as systems thinkers see, who develop their own personal mastery, and who learn how to surface and restructure mental models, collaboratively. Given the influence of organizations in today's world, this may be one of the most powerful steps toward helping us . . altering not just what we think but our predominant ways of thinking. In this sense, learning organizations may be a tool not just for the evolution of organizations, but for the evolution of intelligence. (1990, p. 367)

Yet, as society and organizations evolve from parts to interconnectedness, are leaders and leadership theories truly leading the way? Are our organizational and social leaders anachronisms? It would appear that it is time that today's successful practice of leadership be grounded in clearly articulated leadership theory.

Leadership.

There has been an increasing interest in the ethical dimensions of leadership and leadership as *a process*, a diversion from the industrial paradigm of trait, situational, or "great man" theories. The hierarchical, command-and-control authoritarian approach to leadership seems to be inadequate in its ability to address the myriad of complex issues facing today's society. As we move into the postindustrial era of complex change, and information available to everyone, the process of leadership apparently had to change as well in order to tap into the creative energy of everyone in the organization.

The movement has been away from leadership as a person to leadership as a process, based on relationships with the people in the leadership dynamic. Burns (1978) believes that this process "lies in seeing that the most powerful influences consist of deeply human relationships in which two or more persons engage with one another. It lies in a more realistic, more sophisticated understanding of power, and of the often far more consequential exercise of mutual persuasion, exchange, elevation, and transformation—in short, of leadership. . . . We must see power and leadership as not things (or people) but as *relationships*" (p.11).

The leadership scholar who pioneered the leadership process theory was James MacGregor Burns (1978). He defined leadership as two different relationships, transactional and transforming. Joseph Rost (1991) and other scholars have built on Burn's definition to further define postindustrial leadership as a relationship.

Burns.

Burns's definition of transactional leadership is about an exchange of "valued things," one thing for another, and seems to imply there is limited information available. In contrast, transforming leadership seeks to satisfy higher needs, engages the full person, and seems to fit the ever expanding knowledge base society. "The result of transforming leadership is a relationship of mutual stimulation and elevation that converts followers into leaders and into moral agents" (p.4). Transforming leadership is concerned with end-values such as equality and freedom, compared to modal values such as fair play and justice. This seems to imply a hierarchy of values.

Burns dedicated a chapter to the "psychological matrix of leadership." He talked about needs and wants in terms of value hierarchy relating to Maslow, Erik Erickson, and Kohlberg's stages of moral development. He stated that, "It is in the congruence of the levels and other motivations, and of the stages of moral development, that leadership is animated, politicized, and enlivened with moral purpose" (1978, p. 73). Burns indicates that the process of transforming leadership is bi-causal. If leaders, reflecting higher-level

41

values vied for followers moving toward more socially responsible levels, "leadership itself tends to move on to still broader and 'higher' values" (p. 44).

Burns goes on to say, "a congruence between the need and value hierarchies would produce a powerful potential for the exercise of purposeful leadership. When these hierarchies are combined with stage theories, for example, Erikson's eight psycho-social stages of man . . . leadership, with its capacity to exploit tension and conflict, finds an even more durable foundation" (p. 44).

The leadership relationship then becomes a matter of people inducing each other to be aware or conscious of what they feel. "To feel their true needs so strongly, to define their values so meaningfully that they can be moved to purposeful action . . . Values exist only when there is consciousness" (p.44).

Finally, Burns indicated that both transactional and transforming leadership could contribute to human purpose. Transactional realizes individual goals; transforming is more connected to end-values such as liberty, justice, and equality. But, in a concluding statement Burns argued that although "transforming leaders 'raise' their followers up through levels of morality, insufficient attention to means can corrupt the ends" (p. 426). This seems to be a critical statement of the insufficiency of his leadership definitions. Other than this statement, Burns seems to be alluding to leadership as transcendence, in terms of the process of becoming and reaching for something greater.

Rost.

Burns's work was further defined and interpreted by Joseph C. Rost, author of *Leadership for the 21st Century* (1991). Rost introduced his readers to the concept of post-industrial leadership. Rost defined post-industrial leadership as an "influence relationship among leaders and followers who intend real change that reflects their mutual purposes" (1991). He further defines each piece of the definition. He emphasizes Burns's definition that leaders and collaborators form one relationship that is leadership: "they are in the leadership relationship together" (p. 109). Leadership does not exist without relationship.

Relevant to this study is the explanation of real change: "The word real means that the changes the leaders and followers intend must be substantive and transforming" (p. 115). Rost then goes on to explain transforming. Although he agrees with Burns that leadership is transforming, he does not agree that a moral requirement should be included due to the difficulties that morality would pose for a generalizable definition of leadership. Rost's ambitious quest to provide an all-encompassing and resilient definition of leadership necessarily called for the elimination of a statement about the moral aspect due to thedefficulties in determining whose morals are "more" transforming? His example is an excellent one on the issue of abortion: Both sides, "pro-life" and "pro-choice" groups definitely do leadership by engaging in an influence relationship, intending real change around their mutual purpose. But whose morals are "higher"? Thus Hitler and Mother Theresa can both be called leaders. Even though Burns includes Kohlberg's and Maslow's hierarchies in his definition of higher morals, it still might not bridge the gap for Rost. Rost does state that "leadership and transformation, properly conceived, must deal with the reality of human existence as it is lived, wherein changes are variously evaluated and desired. Leadership, properly defined, is about transformation, all kinds of transformations" (p. 126). If we add the component of transcendence, to Rost's definition, does the "reality of human existence" change?

Other leadership authors: Intimations of Transcendence.

William Foster (1989) of Indiana University, a critical leadership theorist, defined the leadership process as the ability of people to relate deeply in the search for a more perfect union. He wrote:

> Leadership is a consensual task, a sharing of ideas and a sharing of responsibilities, where a "leader" is a leader for the moment only, where the leadership exerted must be validated by the consent of the followers, and where leadership lies in the struggles of a community to find meaning for itself. (p. 57)

John P. Dentico (1998), a doctoral candidate in Leadership Studies and founder of *LeadSimm*, in his article "Games Leaders Play: Using Process Simulations to Develop Collaborative Leadership Practices for a Knowledge Based Society," combines Burns, Rost, and Foster's definitions, adds the constituent of the learning organization from Peter Senge, and produces the collaborative leadership process. "Collaborative leadership is the establishment of relationships built on safety, trust and commitment" (p. 7). Can people without similar values establish this relationship?

Bernard M. Bass, at the Center for Leadership Studies in New York, also wrote extensively on transformational leadership. In an article on *The Ethics of Transformational Leadership*, he first makes the distinction between transactional and transformational. He argues, contrary to the critics, that it is the transactional leaders, who are more self-oriented and are more likely to engage in unethical practices. On the other hand, transformational leaders, being socially-oriented, concentrate on terminal values such as integrity and fairness (1996). He concludes that "true transformational leaders identify the core values and unifying purposes of the organization and its members, liberate their human potential, and foster plural leadership and effective, satisfied followers" (p. 15).

Although Bass and Burns's treatment of transformational leadership seem similar, Richard A. Couto, of the Jepson School of Leadership Studies, begs to differ. He claims that Bass's development of transformational leadership differs substantially from Burns's original conceptualization of transforming leadership (1996). Bass, Couto argues, uses the term "transformational leadership" rather than transforming leadership, implying the subtle change within a process in which a leader participates to a state of being or character of a leader. Therefore, this study will use Burns's definition for transforming leadership.

Robert K. Greenleaf in Servant Leadership, *A Journey into the Nature of Legitimate Power and Greatness* (1975), wrote about the leader as servant. The concept emerged after he had been involved with colleges and universities during the period of campus turmoil in the late 1960s and early 1970s. The servant-leader is one who is servant first and acts with integrity, foresight, intuition, a dedication to consensus, and a sense of history. But servant-leadership is first about deep identity within the servant, who then makes a conscious choice to lead. For Greenleaf, servant-leadership begins with an enlargement of identity, followed by behaviors. Even though his theories are about the individual, he did mention that the leader becomes the follower and vice versa. He also talked about the importance of spirit. He turned to the root of the word *religio*, "to rebind," to explain his understanding of the purpose of religion: "To bridge the separation between persons and the cosmos, to heal the widespread alienation, and to reestablish men and women in the role of servants—*healers*—of society" (p. 25). Greenleaf also talked about the importance of inward grace. "I suggest these five words—beauty, momentaneity, openness, humor, and tolerance—as marking some dimensions of a life style that is rooted in an inward grace" (p. 303). So, while Greenfleaf's definition seems to be about the leader, he clearly states the importance of service to others first. This view is clearly pointing toward transcendence as it needs to reverse the leader/servant role.

Peter Block carried this theme in Stewardship: Choosing Service over Self-Interest (1993). He defined stewardship as "the willingness to be accountable for the well-being of the larger organization by operating in service, rather than in control, of those around us. Stated simply, it is accountability without control or compliance" (p. xx).

Another leadership scholar, Ronald A. Heifetz (1994) in his book Leadership Without Easy Answers, specifically stated that leadership has a moral constituent. Heifetz wrote that ethical consciousness, based on values and morals, is integral to personality and leadership practice. He said that leadership arouses our passions because it is value-laden. Heifetz also wrote, "Leadership inspires hope. . . . The term leadership involves our self-images and moral codes" (p. 13).

In their "Ten Commitments of Leadership," Kouzes and Posner (1995) summarized major "trends" in leadership: searching out challenging opportunities, taking risks, envisioning, enlisting others in vision by appealing to values, collaborating, empowering, modeling the way, achieving small wins, recognizing individuals, and celebrating team accomplishments. Although they believe that leadership is a reciprocal process, they are still appealing to the "great man syndrome" by appealing to an individual as the leader.

Summary

Leadership seems to be moving from "the leader" to people in relationship. Mutuality based on resonating values (good or bad) intensity of movement toward a goal, controlled or governed by transcendence seems to be an emerging key theme. There is a clear movement from transactional to transforming leadership as most effective.

Lisa Aldon

SECTION 2

The Path on the Left: A Brief History of Religion and

Spirituality

(Modern to Postmodern)

Modern

The archives of history are littered with an untold number of dead who were purged in the name of God: victims of the Crusades, the Spanish and French Inquisitions, Lutheranism, Hinduism, and fundamentalism, to name a few. In the year 1500, Europe, recognized as the center of a new civilization spreading quickly to other lands, was still ruled by religion and the values of the church. "Just as men began to feel that to describe society in terms of orders with legally distinct right and obligations no longer expressed its reality, so also they ceased to feel so sure that religion upheld a particular social hierarchy" (Robert, 1993, p. 448).

Lisa Aldon

Postmodern

The sacred texts and traditions of world religions reveal similar themes. Huston Smith's (1991) universally acclaimed work, *The World's Religions: A Guide to Our Wisdom Traditions,* provides a comprehensive, intellectual, and spiritual journey of encounters with Eastern and Western wisdom traditions. Smith's worldview of religions and wisdom traditions seems to be summarized in Confucius's project for harmonizing social relationships in ancient China:

> Having noted there that the task of becoming fully human involves transcending (sequentially egoism, nepotism, parochialism, ethnocentrism and chauvinistic nationalism), we must now add a final step. It involves transcending isolating, self-sufficient humanism as well. In it fullness, humanity "forms one body with Heaven, Earth, and the myriad things." (p. 117)

Smith (1991) drew conclusions about reality and how life should be lived. He wrote about ethics (avoid murder, thieving, lying and adultery), virtues (humility, charity, and veracity), vision (belonging to the whole, the universe is better than our sensibilities discern), and reality (steeped in ineluctable mystery) (p. 454).

In his book *Forgotten Truth*, Smith summarized the world's wisdom in one phrase: "a hierarchy of being and knowing" (in Wilber, 1996, p. 42).

Women's Spirituality

One of the major movements within this path is feminist spirituality. The feminist spirituality movement is one of the most fascinating religious phenomena of the past 20 years. With roots and branches in many places, including neopaganism, political feminism, Jewish and Christian feminism, the New Age, and Native American spirituality, feminist spirituality has emerged as a sociological phenomenon in its own right. It is religiously innovative, always pushing beyond tradition and often leaving it behind in its search for spiritual resources that will prove powerful and transforming for women (Portfield, 1980, p.13).

53

A review of literature by prominent feministic writers such as R. Portfield (1980), S. Anderson and P. Hopkins (1991), T. Frankiel (1990), U. King (1994), C. Spretnak (1994), and C. Matthews (1992), with psychologists C. Gilligan (1982, 1993), and H. Luke (1995) revealed the following predominant themes: (1) relationship—to everything women do and who they are, women only know themselves in relation to others; (2) process—spirituality is about the journey, both inward and external, not the destination; (3) the Goddess—the notion of the divine feminine is empowering not only to women but to men as well, accepting this part of themselves; (4) inward journey—the sacred was found within, by going inward to discover their identities and their personal relationships with God; (5) connectedness—not only to themselves and each other but to the Divine and Mother Earth.

Summary

Key themes are found in both the religious and spirituality literature: the issue of transcendence as paramount to becoming fully human; interconnectedness of self to others, Earth, and spirit; loving thy neighbor as thyself; and a movement from an outward God to and inward God.

SECTION 3

The Abyss Between and The Bridges Across

Chapter One outlined some of the issues in today's society depicted as "the abyss." They include our demoralized society, children killing children, global economic collapse, a nation confronting morality in leadership, global warming, environmental devastation, and on and on. And yet there is now, more than ever, especially in the United States, a spiritual "enlightenment" movement. This paradox seems to become more confusing, and the abyss appears deeper, day by day. But attempts to bridge the abyss, resolve the paradox, have been ongoing since the paths diverged. Humanistic science, self-exploration, adult development, and spirituality have offered some sort of foundation for reaching out to something greater, or searching for meaning. Perhaps what is most absent is an understanding of transcendence and its potential role in bridging the gap.

Bridges - Humanistic Science, Self-Exploration, Adult Development, Spirituality

Richard Bernstein (1983), a philosopher of hermeneutics, the philosophy of textual interpretation, wrote: "Most contemporary philosophers have been in revolt against the Cartesian framework [of science]" (p. ix). He added that modern philosophers and psychologists reject the Newtonian scientific vision, saying it is mechanistic and fractures nature and human nature. The literature of 20th century existential philosophers is built upon the foundation of George W. F. Hegel's (1977), *Phenomenology of Spirit*, which is concerned with *dasein* (being) and takes a moral woldview, or a human spirit worldview.

Existential philosophers argue that human beings by nature are morally responsible, intentional, passional, spiritually free, and one with self and nature. Philosophers William James (1987), Martin Burber (1958), Paul Ricoeur (1984, 1988, and 1992), Pierre Teilhard de Cardin (1959), as well as psychologists Alfred Adler (1959), Carl Jung (1984), Abraham H. Maslow (1970), Viktor E. Frankl (1969), Milhaly Csikszentmihalyi (1993), and Stanislav Groff (1993) are all existential humanists whose worldview is of knowledge as human or spirit knowledge.

Ken Wilber (1995) begs to differ. He wrote: "If you look at the major theorists and critics of the rise of Modernity—such as Hegel, Weber, Habermas, Taylor, Foucault—a surprisingly consistent picture emerges . . . humans became 'objects of information, never subject in communication' . . . [it] produced the dehumanized humanism" (p. 270).

Another bridge is one that focuses on the further understanding of adult development. James Zullo (1966) discussed this topic in a paper he presented at a leadership conference at the University of San Diego. In "Leadership and Adult Development: Postindustrial Paradigms and Parallels," he argued that three convergent areas of research in adult development today are most aligned with a post-industrial leadership of process, relationships, mutual purpose, and transformational change. Of the three, Zullo believes the research most aligned with these concepts looks at the centrality of power and intimacy in the life story. He also points to the research of Robert Kegan, who argues that we are "meaning-makers" and that development is shaped by balancing the two polar motivating forces in adult life: independence and inclusion. And thirdly, Zullo cites the research on women's adult development, which hails affiliation, attachment, and connectedness as hallmarks of adult maturity. Zullo concludes with the statement that "both leadership studies and adult development are in their creative and productive years, struggling to find ways to live out a generativity script that will enhance the quality of our lives as a human community" (p.9).

Many scholars of leadership have stated in one way or another that a fundamental route to effective leadership is through self-knowledge. Stephen Covey (1989), Joseph Jaworski (1996), and Bolman and Deal (1995) all talk about personal development and the journey to better leadership.

It seems many leadership writers have also felt the effects of the abyss. The latest leadership books focus on words like soul, heart, spirit, Jesus, and yes, even love. Bolman and Deal (1995) offer a good example: "Heart, hope, and faith, rooted in soul and spirit, are necessary for today's managers to become tomorrow's leaders, for today's sterile bureaucracies to become tomorrow's communities of meaning, and for our society to rediscover its ethical and spiritual center" (p. 12). Eric Klein and John Izzo (1997), editor Jay Conger (1994), Dorthy Marcic (1997), Ken Blanchard and Michael O'Connor (1997), David Whyte (1994), Margaret J. Wheatley (1992/1994), and editor Larry C. Spears (1998) all discuss bringing spirit and soul into corporate culture. Covey seems to summarize the reason for the movement:

> A great movement is taking place throughout the world today. Its roots, I believe, are to be found in two powerful forces. One is the dramatic globalization of markets and technology. And in a very pragmatic way, this tidal wave of change is fueling the impact of the second force: timeless, universal principles that have governed, and always will govern, all enduring success, especially those principles that give 'air' and 'life' and creative power to the human spirit that *produces* value in markets, organizations, families, and most significantly, individuals' lives. (Spears, Ed., 1998, p. xi)

As the preceding sections describe, the two paths have exhausted their evolutionary potential as people searched for bridges or threads to tie the two together. One model seems not only to bring the two paths together, but to provide a foundation for the future that honors both views. This model maps the stages of human development while synthesizing Western psychology and Eastern spiritual traditions.

Ken Wilber, one of the leading theoreticians of consciousness and a transpersonal psychologist, has developed a "full spectrum" model based on the premise that human development unfolds in predictable stages that extend beyond those recognized by most Western psychologists. Only by moving successfully through each stage is it possible to develop a healthy sense of individuality and ultimately to experience a broader identity that both transcends and includes the separate self.

Wilber's central goal has been to objectively document the stages of consciousness development, including those beyond the ego levels described by Western psychology. Wilber's work is drawn from a broad group of great thinkers and sages, including Sigmund Freud,

Carl Jung, R. D. Laing, Jean Piaget, Lawrence Kohlberg, Carol Gilligan, Krishnamurti, Ramana Maharishi, Sri Aurobindo, and the Buddha.

Wilber's model of consciousness development begins with the pre-personal stages of infancy, extends through the personal or ego levels, and continues up to the transpersonal or highest stages of transpersonal realization. He states that the stages of human development unfold in a predictable, consistent sequence. Even after one reaches the highest stage of personality development—the fully integrated ego described by Freud and others—Wilber argues that it is possible to cultivate equally well delineated stages of transpersonal development. At the same time, the higher stages always have access to the lower stages. Each succeeding level has all the capacities of the previous level, and adds to it, transcending in relation to the previous one. The previous stage's limitations are negated, not the stage itself. Each stage transcends and includes the previous stages (Schwartz, 1995).

Wilber's model explains how it is possible to simultaneously experience both a separate self and a sense of unity or oneness with a larger whole. One is an individual, yet feels part of society. "Mysticism is just the even larger identity of also feeling part of the cosmos at large, and thus finding even greater meaning and value" (Wilber in Schwartz, 1995, p. 535).

In order to further understand the concept of consciousness, a broader definition must be explored. To be sure, consciousness is a difficult concept to define. Joseph Campbell described it in terms of energy: "I have a feeling that consciousness and energy are the same thing somehow. Where you really see life energy, there's consciousness . . . the whole process is consciousness" (p.14). Other definitions include the ability to know one exists and the ability to perceive that one has thoughts, sensory input, and a force or energy that transcends one's physical being and connects humans, plants, animals, everything.

Jenny Wade (1996), another consciousness theorist, offers a more comprehensive explanation. She argues that in order to define consciousness, we must look to such fields as religion, philosophy, neurology, and psychology. These fields focus on three basic essentials of consciousness:

1. Consciousness is the experience of being alive. It is inherent in living existence.

2. Consciousness concerns the intersection between private, interior, subjective experience and the objective or outside world. Transcending this boundary is the crux of mysticism, whereas the interrelationship between what's in here and what's out there forms the thrust of conventional Western developmental models.

3. Memory is an integral part of conscious experience, binding the moment-to-moment sense of awareness into a coherent pattern that provides the sense of personal continuity, the ongoing sense of self.

Wade concludes that consciousness involves comparisons between perceptions of the outside world and whatever internalized images we have built up over the years regarding the nature of the world around us (p. 5,6).

The evolution of consciousness model presented here is based on the summaries of two theorists, Ken Wilber and Jenny Wade. Between the two, they have studied hundreds of theorists from both

Eastern and Western traditions. It seems, then, that every person—regardless of race, gender, age, ethnicity, social status, religion, culture, or other "boundaries" that keep people apart—is going through an evolution of consciousness. Just knowing that, we can begin to look at others and ourselves as part of the whole.

Stage one is marked by the newborn's first capacities for sensation and perception. Stage two is when the development of impulses, emotions, and the capacity for thinking emerge, between the ages of one and three. In stage three, usually from ages three to six, the child begins to use symbols and concepts. Stage four is when the child begins to take on the role of others and performs rule-based tasks (around age six or seven). Stage five, the highest level of development most Westerners reach, is marked by the capacity for rational understanding, introspective thinking, deductive reasoning, and socially acceptable behavior; this stage usually starts around ages twelve to fourteen.

Only the first five stages are age dependent; those that follow are not. Stage six, Wilber concluded, represents the highest potential stage of personal development. It is characterized by a more iterated form of thinking, including the ability to synthesize concepts, connect ideas, and relate truths to one another. It is also the first stage at which a genuine mind-body integration occurs. In stage seven, the psychic stage, one develops psychic capacities, marking the beginning stages of transpersonal awareness. Wilber calls stage eight the subtle level, referring to the notion that there are processes of consciousness more subtle than everyday, outer-directed experience. Stage nine, the causal level, is not just a union of soul and spirit, but "pure Spirit." Lastly, Wilber explains a tenth level of "non-duality," a one with everything and nothing (Schwartz, 1995).

CHAPTER THREE

Introduction to the Model of the Evolution of

Consciousness

I have taken what I consider to be the best of Wilber's and Wade's evolution of consciousness theories and integrated them into a relatively lean model. The other two consciousness models are more comprehensive. For example, the other models include pre-birth/after-death stages of consciousness. But, for the purpose of this thesis, I have simplified it to provide a clear description of the evolution of consciousness upon which concepts of transcendence will rest.

This model seems similar to the psychology of self-development, especially in the first few stages. But, further exploration and study reveals the complexity of the stages of consciousness.

To understand this model, we will first look at the *stages* of consciousness simply stated as matter, body, mind, soul, and spirit, beginning with the early stages. Next, we'll examine what Wilber calls the *lines of development* within each stage. The majority of the information will focus on the "middle" stages, since the majority of the adult population is at these stages. Wade documents the *main characteristics* in every stage. I have chosen three from her model for comparison-and-contrast purposes: (1) ultimate value: what the self values the most; (2) self boundaries: how the self defines itself; and (3) locus of control: what the self thinks it has control over.

Stages

Using Wade's terminology—reactive (matter), naïve (body), egocentric (body/mind), conformist (mind), achievement/affiliate (advanced mind), authentic (mind/soul), transcendent (soul), and unity (spirit)—are stages, whole unto themselves and in a hierarchy of progression. These stages also assume expanding awareness.

Figure 1 shows these stages as different colors in a rainbow, each stage whole, unto itself, but as the self progresses, the colors blend into a new color scheme. Typical ages are matched to the corresponding stage.Wilber (1996) refers to these stages as the *basic structure* and uses the analogy of a ladder:

The ladder metaphor is useful because it indicates

that the basic components of consciousness do emerge

in fairly discrete stages, and if you destroy a lower

rung, all the higher rungs go with it. Where the ladder metaphor fails badly is that each higher stage does not actually sit on top of the lower stage but rather enfolds it in its own being, much as a cell enfolds molecules which enfold atoms. (p. 141,142)

Figure 1

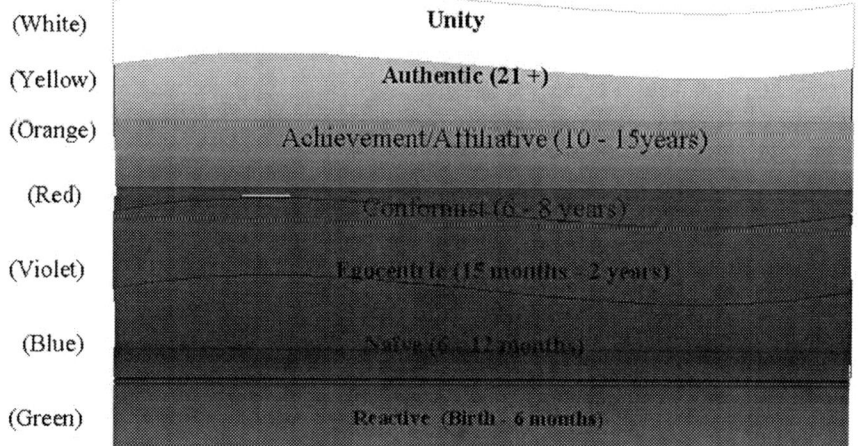

(White)	**Unity**
(Yellow)	**Authentic (21+)**
(Orange)	Achievement/Affiliative (10 - 15years)
(Red)	Conformist (6 - 8 years)
(Violet)	Egocentric (15 months - 2 years)
(Blue)	Naive (6 - 12 months)
(Green)	Reactive (Birth - 6 months)

Stages of Consciousness

Lines of Development

The second major part of the overall model is the lines of development. These transitional or temporary lines are subsequently phased out or replaced. They provide "the view" from any given rung of the ladder. This model will use Wilber's terminology for the major lines of development, which he also calls *transition structures*. He indicates there are many such lines. Within each stage the view of these lines is different. These are further defined as *worldviews* (e.g., archaic, magic, mythic, existential); *self-needs* (e.g., Maslow's hierarchy of safety, belongingness, self-esteem, self-actualization, self-transcendence); *self-identity* (e.g. persona, ego); and *moral stages* (e.g. Kohlberg's preconventional, conventional, post-conventional, post-post-conventional). "Once a particular transition structure is present, it is as important and as real as any enduring structure [stages]; it's just that transitional structures [lines of development] are destined mostly to pass, the others mostly to remain" (Wilber, 1997, p.141).

Most importantly, is the self, or the self-system for integrating and negotiating all the stages and lines of development. I do not believe this is a part of the model; rather, in a sense, it is the model itself. It is the spectrum of consciousness; the self negotiates the lines of development, and it makes the transitions in the evolution of consciousness.

Transition Between Stages

The transition from one stage to the next is a process that Wilber (1996) describes as a *fulcrum*. This is not evident in the model. It is an action within the model. "A fulcrum simply describes the momentous process of differentiation and integration as it occurs in human growth and development. It is simply a crucial fork in the developmental road, and the Self has to deal with that fork. How it does so, in each case decides its subsequent fate" (p. 143-144). Every fulcrum has a 1-2-3 structure. One, the self evolves or develops or steps up to the new level of awareness, and identifies with that level. Two, it then begins to move beyond that level or differentiate from it, or dis-identify with it or transcend it. In order to make the transition, the self goes through a process sensing a discomfort with the state of being, then disassociates, with great loss. In step three, the self then integrates with the next stage. In short, the three steps are as follows: (1)

identify, (2) dis-identify, (3) integrate. Other ways of describing this is fusion, differentiation, integration, *or* embed, transcend, include. This process is a fulcrum of self-development, and there are as many fulcrums of self-development as there are stages of consciousness to negotiate (p. 143). In addition, the self is both the "ground" of every stage and the goal of every stage, guiding, pulling, and directing so that every stage of development is drawn closer to self-realization. Could this fulcrum effect be important to the leadership relationship if it is to be transforming?

Figure 2 integrates the stages of consciousness and the major lines of human development with their corresponding views at each stage.

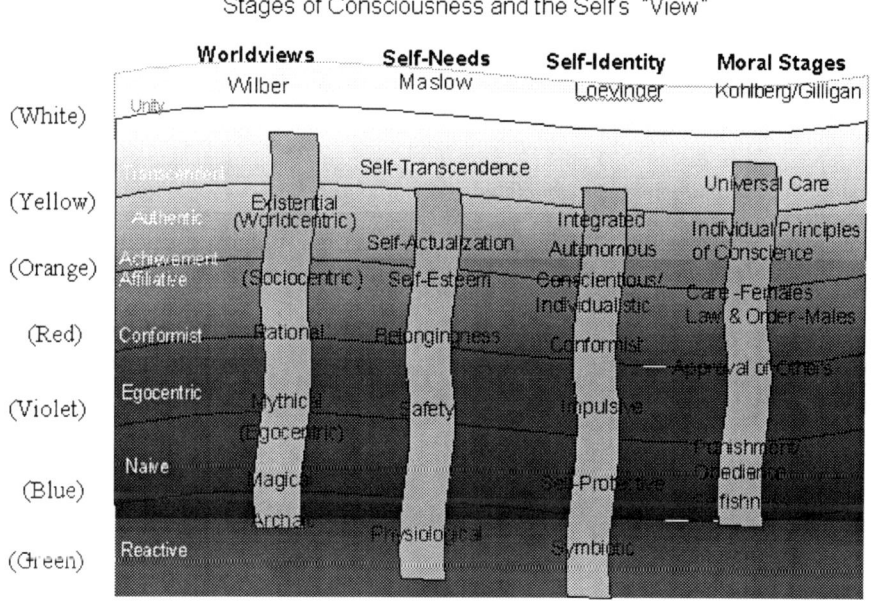

Figure 2

As an example, let's follow one stage all the way through. The Conformist begins to develop in children around age seven. The Conformist is characterized by the capacity to form complex mental rules and to take social roles. Children begin to understand that they are not just a body with impulses and desires, but also a social self among other social selves. As the basic structure emerges, the child's self will face that new rung of awareness, so it must negotiate the fulcrum at that level—the 1-2-3 process. Normally, the self steps into that level of awareness and identifies with it. It has a sense of conforming with these rules and roles; therefore the "self-identity" is conformist. Accordingly, the basic need at this stage is for belongingness, and the self's moral stance centers on the conventional approval of others.

The Model: Definition

Reactive

Stage: This stage is from birth of the self (in physical form) to about one year old. The primary motivation is the cessation of discomfort. It is called reactive "to capture its dependence upon environmental factors" (Wade, 1993, p. 74).

Main Characteristics/Lines of Development: The self-need is simply physiological and the self identifies only with symbols at this stage.

Naïve

Stage: This stage is from about one to two years old. The emotional self begins to differentiate itself from the emotional environment. The infant actually expresses as a separate emotional and feeling self at this stage. The infant "wakes up" to the fact that it is a separate self, existing in a separate world.

Wilber's model (in his more simplified version, from about 17 stages to 9) explains the first three stages as physical, phantasmic-emotional, and representational. The first two stages of his model fit closely with the naïve stage. According to Wilber, at this point the infant has established the realistic boundaries of its physical self but it has not yet established the boundaries of its emotional self. Wilber's third or representational stage fits closely with both the reactive stage in that "the self lacks such rule coordination and cannot easily take the role of other" (1983/1990/1996, p.269), and the egocentric stage, in which the person is very egocentric or narcissistic.

Main Characteristics: The ultimate value at this stage is security through ritual. Self-boundaries are permeable and they include

75

people, animals, and things in the environment. The locus of control is external and more competent or powerful other person.

Lines of Development: If adults are in this stage, psychology has named them "neurotic adults." They want to be protected from an imprecisely perceived, but nevertheless insecure, world that "finds expression in a search for a protector or a stronger person upon whom [they] may depend. They fill their lives with ceremonies, rules and formulae, maintaining their equilibrium by avoiding the unfamiliar." (Wade quoting Maslow, p.88). This pre-egonic stage in adults is also characterized by problems with self-awareness. The primary motivation in this stage is physical security and safety at the levels of sustenance, reproduction, and the avoidance of pain and change.

Egocentric

Stage: This stage for most people begins at age two with the formation of a separate self. (All developmental theories start with this stage.) What the child sees is what he thinks. At this point, concepts begin to emerge. The self is now not just a bundle of sensations, impulses, and emotions; it is also a set of symbols and concepts. It begins to enter the linguistic world. It is a time of pain and selfishness that includes high anxiety, paranoia, and egocentrism. Wade (1996) describes it this way: "Having cut itself off from the Terrible Mother and identified with Oedipal Father, the ego creates a split from both the Ground of All Being (Spirit) and the body. The resulting mental ego reduces the body to the merely material, and at the same time elevating itself to the immaterial. The mental ego knows *that* it exists, the problem is that it does not know *what*, if anything it is" (p. 99-100).

Wilber describes this stage (and an additional stage in his model) as representational or representational-mind. The self can think of the past and plan for the future, it can begin to picture things in its mind that are not actually present in its senses. The self is no longer exclusively identified with the emotional level. It identifies with the mental or conceptual self.

Main characteristics: The ultimate value is egonic survival by force and cunning. Self-boundaries are firm, located at the skin. The locus of control is internal, the self for its survival.

Lines of Development: Egocentric individuals believe they are fighting for survival in a hostile world where their needs and ego can be gratified and protected only by being stronger and tougher than other entities. The self-need is safety and the self identity is impulse.

Conformist

Stage: This stage involves the capacity to form mental rules and to take mental roles.

The child finally learns to take the role of other. The typical age group for this stage is around 10–16 years. Alternative possibilities begin to exist. Conceptualization is limited by the absolute and dualistic nature of thinking (right/wrong, good/bad, black/white). The self can also clearly perform rule operations, such as multiplication, division, class inclusion, and so on. As the ego advances beyond the fundamental repression of the previous stage, it builds up more layers of illusion in reaction to its separation from the Ground of All Being, which is considered the fundamental delusion of human existence by esoteric traditions (Wade, 1996, pp.127-128). This also extends to alienation from the body because the egoic processes continue to emphasize mental capacities and abstraction as a way of mapping the world, rather than direct participation (p.129). As the ego's strength increases, it becomes even more alienated from the spiritual and involved in the mental world of its own ideas as a necessary part of human evolution.

Main characteristics: The ultimate value is control. Self-boundaries are at the skin. Locus of control is external, the referent group.

At this point, I would like to introduce a fourth important characteristic: *concept of other*. At this stage, people are similar to the Self, possessing their own point of view, primarily judged by externals, especially group identifications by virtue of rules and roles creates social inequities that are right and just. How we view others is an important factor in the leadership relationship.

Lines of Development: As stated earlier, the self has a sense of conforming with these rules and roles, therefore the "self-identity" is conformist. And for the same reason, the basic need is for belongingness. And the self's moral stance centers on the conventional approval of others.

Achievement/Affiliative

At this point there are two different "paths" along the same stage—Achievement and Affiliative. "Although stages are invariant up to the Conformist level, people move from there to either Affiliative or Achievement consciousness, depending on enculturation and [brain] hemispheric dominance" (Wade, 1996, p.134). Both stages are equal in terms of complexity even though their expression is different: individual achievement or social relatedness. Either stage could come after Conformist depending on physiological, gender, and cultural factors. At this stage on either path, true introspection becomes possible as the interior world, for the first time, opens up before the mind's eye. It is the first structure that can not only think about the world but think about thinking; hence, it is the first structure that is clearly self-reflective and introspective and can imagine possibilities.

Note: Wilber does not make a distinction between Achievement and Affiliative. He calls this stage *formal-reflexive*. The person begins to imagine different possible worlds. "It's the age of reason and revolution" (Wilber, 1996, p. 186).

Stage: Achievement. Procedural knowledge is separate knowing. "In Separate knowledge, truth, though not immediately accessible, is found through deliberate, systematic analysis that occurs while holding the self apart from the object of inquiry. The heart of Separate knowledge is critical thinking, doubt and reason" (Wade, 1996, p.140). Achievement consciousness represents a higher degree of egoic separation than conformism. "In the face of spiritual separation and the sense of personal finitude, the mental ego seeks to create permanence in the world of ideas through planning and achievements that can be materially translated into personal monuments" (p. 145).

Lines of Development: At this stage, both Achievement and Affiliative have sociocentric worldviews. They have high self-esteem and are conscientious. But, again, the moral stance is more around the ethic of justice for Achievement than the "ethic of care" for Affiliative. (These are the psychologist Carol Gilligan's terms for describing the way the different genders handle moral issues.)

Main characteristics: The ultimate value is power to be better than others and have them know it. Self-boundaries are at the skin. Locus of control is internal, the self for self-esteem. Concept of other recognizes that people are similar, possessing their own point of view but not similar in the ability to achieve; achievers will be rewarded with the good things in life (usually defined materially) over the less capable; more powerful, successful people are admired; people without the measures of success are discounted, others may be exploited within socially acceptable limits.

Stage: Affiliative. Procedural knowledge is Connected knowing. "Connected knowledge develops through intimacy and equality between the self and the object of discourse, based on empathetic understanding. Thinking is within dialectical constraints. Connected knowers can criticize a system, but only according to the terms and the standards of the system." (p.148)

Main characteristics: The ultimate value is being needed. Self-boundaries are at the skin. Locus of control is external, chosen like-minded peer groups. Concept of other: people are similar, possessing their own point of view; sharing information about one's inner life with others will lead to a consensus-based community; differences are superficial, everyone is fundamentally equal; differences and conflict are threatening; people need to be helped by being in close relationships.

Authentic

Stage: Authentic consciousness resolves both the Achievement and the Affiliation dilemmas, using a synergistic blend of both solutions that is greater than the sum of its parts. This stage represents the height of most conventional developmental theory. It is markedly free of the ego defenses seen prior to this level, so that persons at this level are able to experience and express themselves fully. "It is called Authentic not because it is the first legitimate stage, but because selfhood is undistorted by ego" (Wade, 1996, p.161).

Main characteristics: The ultimate value is fulfilling personal mission, even if not understood. Self-boundaries are at the skin. Locus of control is internal-personal growth. Concept of other: very little ego-based distortion, true empathy, respect for personal agency, diversity and autonomy of others, relatively free of conformity to social expectations.

Lines of Development: At this stage, the view is worldcentric or global. You are no longer egocentric nor are you ethnocentric. At the existential level, you are not yet in the transpersonal, but you are no longer totally anchored in the personal: the whole personal domain has started to become profoundly meaningless. The self at this stage is more often than not profoundly unhappy. It is integrated and autonomous and miserable. It has tasted everything the personal realm can offer, and it's not enough. "This is the soul for whom all desires have become thin and pale and anemic. This is a soul who, in facing existence squarely, is thoroughly sick of it. This is a soul for whom the personal has gone totally flat. This is, in other words, a soul on the brink of the transpersonal" (Wilber, 1996, p. 196). Does this describe the latest "spirituality in the workplace" or "awakening corporate soul" movement? Is this what collaborative leadership is addressing?

In Wilber's model, this is the *vision-logic* stage . He sees it as a type of synthesizing and integrating awareness stage. "We tend to get a very highly integrated personality, a self state can actually inhabit a global perspective and not merely mouth it"(Wilber, 1996, p. 191). This stage is the integration of the mind and the body, a self integrated in its networks of responsibility and service. "Spirit is looking at the world through infinitely wondrous perspectives; it does not mean it has gone blind in the process. This is simply a further de-centering, a further transcendence, another spiral in the evolution against egocentrism" (p.193).

The final stages of consciousness are difficult to summarize. They are based on world mysticism, Jungian psychology, and other information not well known to the main population. I will describe them mainly by using Wade's and Wilber's exact words. But first, to summarize where we've come, Wilber (1996) states:

> We have moved from an identity with the material dimension (stage 1), [reactive] to an identity with the biological dimension (stage 2), [naïve] to an identity with a mental self (stage 3), [egocentric]. At stage 4 [conformist] identity switches from egocentric (or self-bound) to sociocentric (or group-bound). Here your awareness already transcends the merely "individual" aspects. Your very awareness, your very identity, is based upon cultural roles and collective identities and shared values. It is no longer a *body* identity, is a *role* identity. . . With rationality at stage 5, [achievement/affiliative] your identity de-centers or expands once again, this time transcending any merely ethnocentric or sociocentric identity, and finding a worldcentric identity, an identity in the circle of all human beings [authentic]. It's only a small step further to actually experience your central identity, not just

with all human beings, but all living beings. You experience "World Soul" (p.203), [transcendence]. (Authors parentheses).

Transcendent

Stage: Conventional psychology virtually ceases at Authentic consciousness. The last two stages are the transpersonal stages, the superconscious domains. The observing self from the Authentic stage continues to observe into deeper and deeper realms of consciousness. "As consciousness evolution continues, it discloses more and more depth to this observing self. . . . The answer is given by the world's great mystics and sages is that this observing self goes straight to Spirit" (Wilber, 1996, p.197).

Main characteristics: The ultimate value is unity with the Ground of All Being. Self-boundaries are the ego with all its psychic structures; the self is constructed. Locus of control is external regarding grace and power of the Absolute; being at one with reality leads to participation in creating it. Concept of other: others are appreciated for their participation in the Ground of All Being regardless of outward form; great compassion for and identification with all life forms.

Lines of Development: At this point, the lines of development fade into the spirit of everything. The Self is starting to dis-identify with the mind itself, which is why it can witness the mind, see the mind, and experience the mind.

Wilber calls this stage Subtle consciousness and believes these higher levels of consciousness are present as potential in all human beings. "Subtle" simply means processes that are subtler than gross, ordinary, waking consciousness. It involves your own Archetypal form, a union with God or Goddess, a union with Buddha, and so on.

What do you find if you push beyond the mind, into a depth of consciousness that is not confined to the ego or the individual self? What do you find? 'There is a subtle essence that pervades all reality, it is the reality of all that is, and the foundation of all that is. That essence is all. That essence is the real. And thou, thou art that.'(Wilber, 1996, p. 199)

Unity

Stage: The last stage identified in noetic development concerns transcending the desire to lose the self in order to grasp the Absolute.

The most complex known state of consciousness is characterized by the permanent cessation of the motives for becoming. It is the nirvana of Buddhism, the samadhi of yoga, the satori of Zen, the fana of Sufism, the Kingdom of Heaven of Christianity, the shema of Judaism. Attainment of this kind of consciousness causes a permanent alteration in the person's way of being in the world. Desire, attachment, and self-interest die as all egoism is extinguished. (Wade, 1996, p.203)

Main characteristics: There is no ultimate value and no self-boundaries. The Self is the same as Cosmic Consciousness. Locus of control is internal as free will expresses the Ground of All Being and emanates from it. Concept of other: there are no others in the absolute sense; recognition of the bounded selves that exist in the material plane as multiplicities of the One.

Lines of Development: At this stage, there are no lines of development, it's just Self.

Wilber presents two stages in these transpersonal realms: *Casual* and *Nondual*. Casual state can never be seen as an object; this pure Self is pure emptiness, infinitely drenched in the fullness of being, so full that no manifestation can ever begin to contain it. It is called Casual because it is the support or cause or creative ground of all junior dimensions. Creativity is part of the basic ground of the universe, the self-transcending capacity of the universe.

Once we recognize and honor all levels—not just matter, body and mind, but soul and spirit as well—we simultaneously acknowledge all the corresponding modes of knowing. Wilber (1997) puts it this way:

> Not just the eye of flesh, which discloses the
> physical and sensory world, or just the eye of mind,

which discloses linguistic and symbolic world, but also the eye of contemplation, which discloses the soul and spirit. . . . That integral vision is, I submit, the final homecoming, the reweaving of our modern soul with the soul of humanity itself—the true meaning of multiculturalism—so that, standing on the shoulders of giants, we transcend but include, which always means honor, their ever-recurring presence. Uniting ancient wisdom with modern knowledge is thus the clarion call of the integral vision, a beacon in the postmodern wilderness (p. 50).

I believe, with this integral vision as our beacon, the leadership relationship is the process of implementation.

Summary

The "master template" assembled by Wilber, Wade, and others is a comprehensive psychology of matter, body, mind, soul, and spirit. Wilber has identified seven areas of common philosophical ground embraced by virtually all of the great contemplative traditions, West and East.

> First, Spirit or a Supreme Reality exists. Second, it is found within one's self. Third, most of us don't recognize this Spirit because we live with an illusory sense of separateness from others and from the universal ground of all being. Fourth, the path to liberation requires building a broader identity in which the wholly separate sense of self is surrendered. Fifth, if this path is followed to its conclusion, it leads finally to rebirth, or enlightenment—in the form of either a direct experience of the Spirit within or oneness with God. Sixth, this experience marks the end of suffering. And seventh, the natural outgrowth of such enlightenment is a life grounded in compassion and directed toward selfless service. (in Schwartz, 1995, p. 354)

At the highest stage, the statement "love thy neighbor as thyself" is not a moral injunction but a description of a state of consciousness in which you and your neighbor are experienced as one and the same. The path to wisdom, or transcendence in Wilber's model is built around progressively broadening one's boundaries and thus enlarging one's sense of self. "The aim is to remember something of ourselves that we had formerly forgotten. To remember is simply to re-member and re-collect . . . to make whole that which was split and fragmented." (Wilber quoted in Schwartz, 1995, p. 360)

CHAPTER FOUR

Integration of Consciousness Model with Leadership

Theories

Introduction

The focus and intent of Chapter Two was designed to present a literature review that described one or another of two paths of human development. One path was described as the classical scientific and material path; the other was described as the path of traditional religion and spirituality. Both offer disparate explanations of social development from modern to postmodern times. The reason for highlighting these views was to demonstrate wide differences in interpretation of the same historical phenomena, within two distinct frameworks. Various themes were presented to show the great similarity between both frameworks regardless of which path an individual would chose to follow. Additionally, all the major theories of leadership were described and linked to the classical scientific path in order to show a strong relationship absent from a leadership/spirituality linkage. Chapter Three presented a model of individual evolution of consciousness that demonstrated human development unfolding in a predictable and consistent sequence. Chapter Four will provide an integrated perspective using the model of consciousness to provide the reasoning for the inclusion of transcendence and consciousness, i.e. a kind of concrete spirituality, in any future model of leadership. As previously asserted, a future model of leadership must fully support the human desire to transcend, if humankind, including organizations are to become ever more effective.

The Two Paths Depicted

Figure Three shows two paths described in Chapter Two depicted against the waves of societal development delineated by Toffler and Toffler.

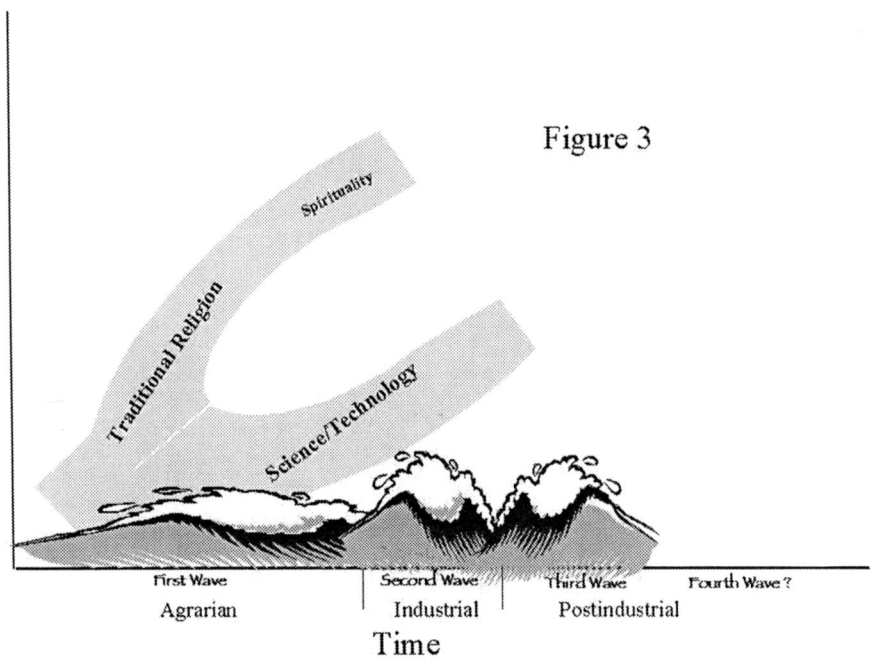

Figure 3

Figure 3

"The first wave of change, the agricultural revolution took thousands of years to play itself out. The second wave, the rise of industrial civilization, took a mere three hundred years" (Toffler and Toffler, 1995, p. 19). According to Toffler and Toffler, we are in the midst of the third wave, set off by the knowledge and global communication revolution. Within this third wave we are experiencing much more than a social change but as Drucker stated, a change in the human condition (1994). Professor William Halal, has termed the level of change in society today as nothing less than the "Second Copernican Revolution" (Halal, 1995) and might be considered tantamount to extra terrestrials visiting our planet. The new civilization changes the ways of working, loving and living; it embraces a new economy and includes an altered consciousness as well (Toffler, et.al. 1995). But, as Toffler goes on to say, history is today, even more accelerated. They estimate the third wave will complete itself in a few decades. If this is so, then we might ask what theories of leadership will evolve and predominate?

Leadership Theories and the Two Paths

Figure Four shows the major leadership theories as they relate to the two paths shown in Figure Three and to the Tofflers' explanation of the waves of societal development. The theories of leadership are shown in approximate relationship to the time wave and path (traditional religion or classical science), when each of these theories was at its height in popularity.

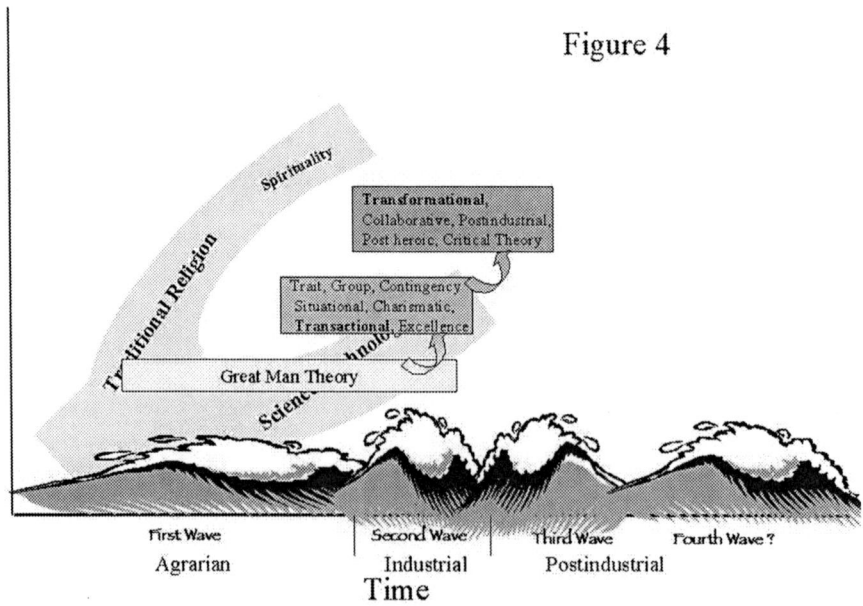

Figure 4

Figure 4

Consciousness: Individual to Society

To project the dimensions of near and far future leadership theory, it is necessary to integrate the spectrum of consciousness into today's most accepted theories. The previous chapter showed that the combined Wilber/Wade model explained consciousness at the individual level. Yet it is clear that Wilber's world view is similar to that of Duane Elgin's societal or planetary model as shown in his seminal work *Awakening Earth, Exploring the Evolution of Human Culture and Consciousness.* Table 1 shows the comparison of the individual stages of consciousness and the societal or planetary stages of consciousness models of Wilber/Wade, and Elgin. For comparison, Maslow and Erickson's hierarchies are also included to ground the model in the work of more traditional human development scholars. This table also includes Toffler's description of the three waves. Elgin's focus on planetary development emerges from enduring wisdom of the world's spiritual traditions as well as from new insights in science. It is a story of human evolution that emerges in a highly purposeful process of development. Just as there are recognizable

99

stages in the movement of an individual from infancy to early adulthood, so, too, there seems to be stages of evolvement that describes our maturation as a species. Elgin wrote,

> We need to draw on our collective wisdom and discover images of the future that awaken our enthusiasm for evolution and mobilize our social energies. By drawing upon the world's growing body of wisdom in biology, anthropology, history, physics, systems theory, comparative religion, and so on, we can begin to disarm the overall direction of human evolution that leads toward our maturity as a planetary civilization. (1995, p. 14).

Maslow's Hierarchy of Needs	Eriksen's Self Identity Model	Wade's (with Wilber) Self's Evolution of Consciousness	Time	Wilber's World View	Elgin (Society)	Toffler & Toffler (Society View)
		Unity			Planetary Wisdom	
Self-Transcendence	Integrated	Transcendent		Existential	Balancing Species Creativity and Unity	
Self-Actualization	Autonomous	Authentic		Worldcentric	Global Bonding	
Esteem	Conscientious Individualistic	Achievement/Affiliative		Sociocentric	Mass Communication and Global Reconciliation	Wave Three
Social	Conformist	Conformist		Rational	Industrial	Wave Two
Safety	Implusive	Egocentric		Mythical	Agricultural	
	Self-Protective	Naive		Archaic/Magical	Hunter/Gatherer	Wave One
Physiological	Symbiotic	Reactive			Archaic Humans	

Table 1

Elgin provides a staged interpretation of the societal development encountered and it is these striations which act as the axes of transcendence for the consciousness model, and are integrated in figure five.

Evolving Leadership Theories

Figure Five now depicts the leadership theories in comparison to the spectrum of consciousness. It seems the theories are evolving a step behind the evolution of the individuals who created them. The movement from "great man" to trait/situational/transactional to collaborative/transforming leadership seems to be an outgrowth and improvement of what leadership practice previously prevailed.

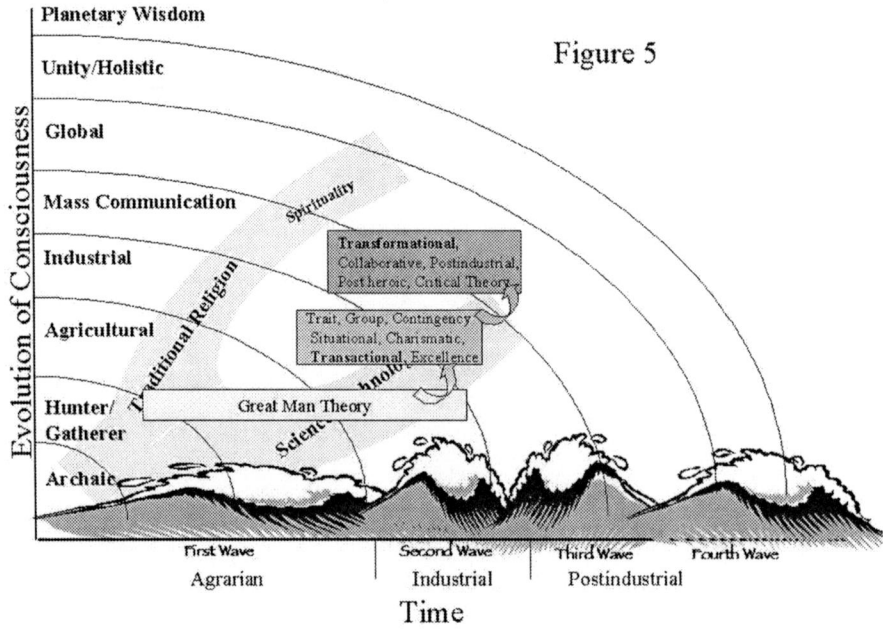

Figure 5

Figure 5

Some characteristics within particular leadership theories can be correlated with the Worldview (Wilber) column in Table 1. The main era of "great man" spans the Mythical and Rational world view which seems to be a close correlation to some described characteristics, i.e. "great man" as leader always seemed to be "larger than life", and have a rational way of approaching issues.

Transactional leadership, to chose one of the main theories during the industrial era seems to closely fit the "manager as leader" definition, an authority relationship between manager and subordinate who coordinate their activities to produce and sell particular goods and/or services. (Rost, 1991).

Transforming leadership seems to straddle the Rational and Sociocentric worldview. This would support Bass's characteristic of transactional leadership as being more self-centered, vs. transforming seen as more sociocentric.

Could it be that organizations that continue to adhere to older theories of the "great man" theory and/or transactional theory will reach a point of non-evolution to failure? Clearly, the practicing management today needs to lean heavily toward collaboration and teaming, i.e. is transformation of the employee, organization and customer, in short, transforming of society itself?

Transcendence leadership theory

A very clear picture of evolution appears with the combination of all of these frameworks and models, holistic in its span and depth.

But, as stated earlier, society continues to be paradoxical, continuing down two vastly different and distinct paths, science/technology and traditional religious beliefs. But, as shown in Figure Five, both paths can be considered as interstates on the overall map of consciousness.

Leadership theories play a quintessential role in this roadmap. The leadership process can provide the opportunity in which individuals and therefore society will realize its evolution and its transcendence. No other process we have can honor the individual, interact within a group or communities, and rally around the mutual purpose for transforming, society through transcendence. Where else can we realize this, but within managed institutions. Drucker, in a recent article on the New Paradigm of Management, states "The center of modern society, economy and community is not technology, it is not information, it is not productivity. The center of modern society is the managed institution . . . The institution, in short, does not simply exist within and react to society. It exists to produce results on and in society" (Drucker, 1998, p. 176). Elgin declared that "the quality of our shared attention is the most precious resource that we possess as a human family and is basic to our evolution as a species" (1996, p. 19).

The reality of persons as transcendent has the potential of enhancing, even evolving leadership theory into the 21st century. Some leadership scholars are looking toward Robert Greenleaf's servant leadership as the next step in the logical progression of evolving theories. The connection between servant and transcendence is, transcendence provides the awareness/consciousness for the servant leader to develop better ways to lead and grow.

John J. Gardiner, author of *Quite Presence: the Holy Ground of Leadership*, feels servant leadership emphasizes transcendence.

> Changing the underlying structure of our perceptions to seeing with eyes of wholeness our fundamental interconnections with eachother and with all of life is at the heart of the world's major religion and the modern sciences of biology and physics, is also at the heart of the transformation. The new leadership must move from the transformational emphasis of James MagGregor Burns to the transcendent emphasis of Robert K. Greenleaf. (Spears, Ed., 1997, p. 121)

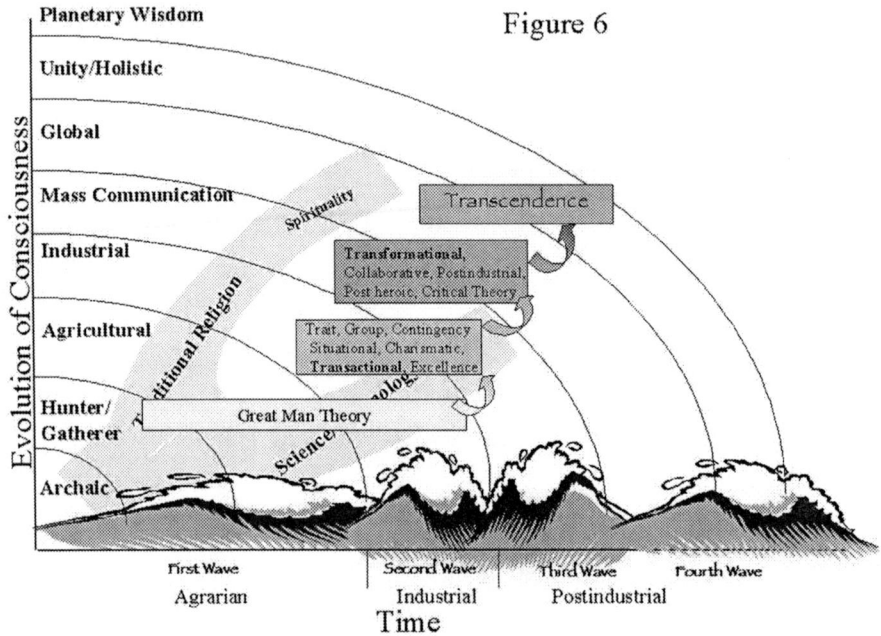

Figure 6

Finally, Figure six, depicts three major themes of this thesis. First, it unequivocally recognizes that every individual is evolving. "The central claim of the perennial philosophy – the esoteric or inner core of the wisdom religions - is that men and women can grow and develop (or evolve) all the way up the hierarchy to Spirit itself" (Wilber, 1997, p. 39). As individuals evolve, so to does the society in which individuals create communities. Second, it offers a comprehensive view of how we overall are evolving throughout history. Finally, it shows that the two paths, science/technology and spirituality continue to be split within the overall model and each are likely to continue to attract advocates. Therefore, whichever way one chooses to look at the future, the ultimate resolution of this paradox or the way in which to rid ourselves of the abyss, is transcendence.

As we overlay leadership theories within either framework of the path metaphor, or the evolution of consciousness model, it shows a similar story. The theories follow more of an overall human behavior development. The depiction of leadership theories is both progressive and cumulative. So, as we look into the future, what is the next step? Or, as we stand on the shoulders of giants, what do we see?

Evolving, Healing, Honoring

If transcendence is included in the leadership theories, a synergistic, bridging process of honoring the self <u>and</u> the many, in a "spiritual humanism" could be possible.

The energy and creativity released by combining a balance concern for the material and consciousness aspects of life are not simply additive, they are synergistic . . . A co-evolutionary perspective reveals

107

an elevated pattern and purpose to human evolution
that can guide us toward a future bursting with creative
possibility (Elgin, p. 17).

Figure Seven depicts a possible future of the main themes
presented in this thesis, the paths, leadership and consciousness.

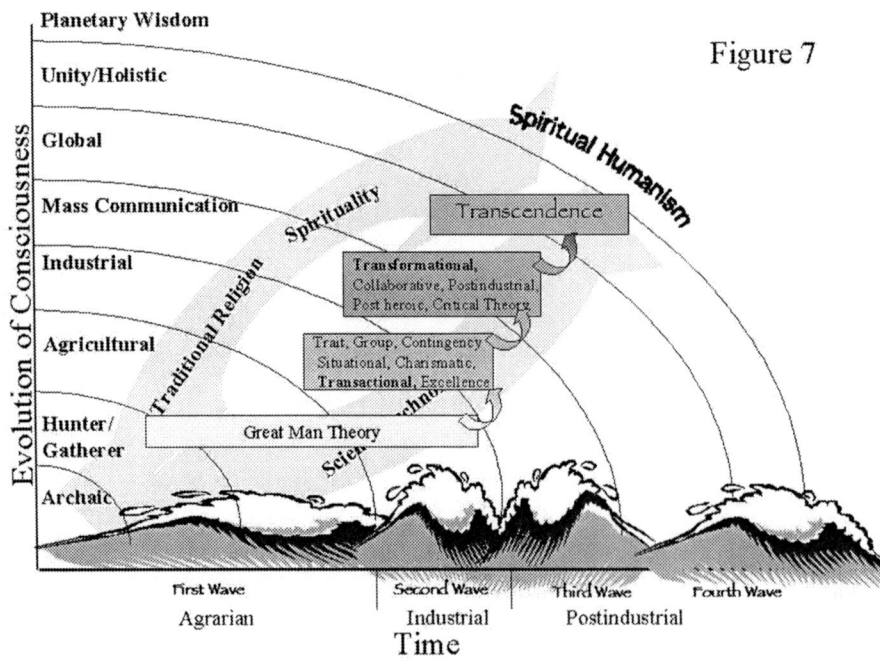

Figure 7

Utilizing transcendence as a fundamental element in the
leadership process, and honoring the best of the two paths,
spirituality, reflecting on enlightenment (without cultural tyranny) and

the strength of the individual freedom (without the tyranny of "anti-soul") will become a viable mode of human transformation.

Riding the crest of the fourth wave with spiritual humanism as our surfboard, can there be a more exciting ride?

CONCLUSION

This thesis is an offer to all humankind to better understand each other within a common frame of reference. Every sentient being is going through the process of evolution, therefore every sentient being is capable of transcendence, from body, to mind, to soul and to Spirit. Each person is a vitally important and unique agent in the process of planetary evolution. Humanity can reach no higher than the social fabrics that can be woven together from the synergy of the strength of our individual lives (Elgin, 1995). But we seem to fear discovering the godlike in ourselves, for that discovery implies great responsibility for our circumstances. As Nelson Mandela stated:

Our deepest fear is not that we are inadequate.

Our deepest fear is that we are powerful beyond measure.

It is our light, not our darkness that most frightens us.

We ask ourselves, who am I to be brilliant, gorgeous, talented and fabulous.

Actually, who are you not to be? You are a child of God. . .

We were born to make manifest the glory of God that is within us.

It's not just in some of us. It's in everyone.

And as we let our own light shine, we unconsciously give others permission to do the same.

As we are liberated from our own fear, our presence automatically liberates others (1994).

Each of us, individually is this extraordinary complexity of the beautiful tapestry of consciousness. With this mindful knowledge and soulful knowledge we can begin to realize that we are all connected. When we look into one another's eyes, and ourselves, we need to realize we are looking at Spirit, the God of our fathers and the Goddess of our mothers. Deep down, in our heart of hearts, in our integrity of Being, we all want the same thing – to be loved, to be connected and to give love.

And whatever the form of your own resurrection, you will arise, driven not by the Great Search, but by your Great Duty, your limitless Dharma, the manifestation of your own highest potentials, and the world will begin to change, because of you. And you will never flinch, and you will never fail in that great Duty, and you will never turn away, because simple, ever-present awareness will be with you now and forever, even unto the ends of the worlds, because now and forever and endlessly forever, there is only Spirit, only intrinsic awareness, only the simple awareness of just this, and nothing more (Wilber, 1997, p. 300).

Now is the time to invest our enthusiasm in the conscious co-evolution of life on Earth, for it is only through our individual awakening that the Earth will heal as well. We have to recall a memory that we can't quite remember, but our spirit never forgot.

Limitations of the Study

Because this study was a general orientation overview, the details of how, what and why were not addressed.

Suggested Further Research

Some suggestions for future study would be how consciousness specifically effects the leadership process. For example, in transitioning from one stage to the next, (the fulcrum), can the leadership process help in advancing stages? Can the leadership process become a fulcrum? If so, how?

How could leadership be defined as a transcendent process? Could core values be different (Burns/Pienta hierarchy of values)? Could a mutual purpose be sustainability for our children's children?

REFERENCES

Adler, A. (1959). Understanding human nature. New York: The Bobs-Merrill Company, Inc.

Anderson, S. R. & Hopkins, P. (1991). The feminine face of god. New York, NY: Batam Books.

Bass, B. M., (1985). Leadership and performance beyond expectations. New York: The Free Press.

Bass, B. M., (1996). The ethics of transformational leadership. New York: State University of New York.

Bell, D. (1973). The coming of the post-industrial society, a venture in social forcasting. New York: Basic Books, Inc.

Bellah, R. N., Madsen, R., Sullivan, W. M., Swidler, A., Tipton, S.M. (1985). Habits of the heart. New York: Harper & Row.

Bellah, R. N., Madsen, R., Sullivan, W. M., Swidler, A., Tipton, S.M. (1991). The good society. New York: Vintage Books.

Bernstein, R. Jo. (1983). Beyond objectivism and relativism. Philadelphia: University of Pennsylvania Press.

Blanchard, K. & O'Connor, M. (1997), Managing by values. San Francisco: Berrett-Koehler.

Block, P. (1993, 1996). Stewardship, choosing service over self-interest. San Francisco: Berrett-Koehler.

Bolman, L. G. & Deal, T.E., (1995). Leading with soul, an uncommon journey of spirit. San Francisco: Jossey-Bass Inc.

Buber, M. (1958/1987). I and thou. (R. G. Smith, Trans.). New York: Macmillan Publishing. (Original work published 1952).

Burns, J. M. (1978). Leadership. New York: Harper & Row.

Bergquist, W. The postmodern organization, mastering the art of irreversible change. San Francisco: Jossey-Bass Inc.

Cambell, J. (1988). The power of myth. Flowers, B. S. Ed. New York: Doubleday.

Cassel, R. N. (1973). Psychological aspects of human freedom. Psychology, 10(4), 3739.

Capra, F., & Steindle-Rast, D. (1992). Belonging to the universe. New York: Harper Collins.

Capra, F. (1980). The turning point. New York: Bantam Books.

Couto, R.A., (1996). Social capital and leadership. Article prepared for the Transformational Leadership Section of the Kellogg

Leadership Study Project of the Center for Political Leadership and Participation at the University of Maryland.

Csikszentmihalyi, M. (1993). The evolving self. New York: Harper Perennial.

Csikszentmihalyi, M. (1993). Optimal experience, psychological studies of flow in consciousness. England: Cambridge Press.

Dentico, J.P., (1998). Games leaders play: using process simulations to develop collaborative leadership practices for a knowledge based society. Article in Leadership in Management.

dc Tocquevill, A. (1990). Democracy in america (Vol. 1-2). (H. Reeve, Trans., and F Browen & P. Bradly, Eds.) New York: Vintage Books.

Drucker, P.F. (1994). (pp. 40-64). Atlantic Monthly, November.

Drucker, P.F. (1998). (pp. 2-16) New paradigm of management.

Elgin, D. (1993). Awadening earth, exploring the evolution of human culture and consciousness. New York, William Morrow and Company, Inc.

Foster, W. (1989). Toward a critical practice of leadership. In J. Smyth (Ed.), <u>Critical perspectives on educational leadership</u> (pp. 40-65). London: Falmer.

Frankiel, T. (1990). <u>The voice of sarah</u> San Francisco: Harper

Frankl, V.E., (1962). <u>Man's serch for meaning: An introduction to logotherapy.</u> Boston: Beacon Press.

Gardiner, J. J. (1997) In Spears, L.C. Ed., <u>Insights on leadership, service, stewardship, spirit, and servant-leadership.</u> New York: John Wiley and Sons, Inc.

Gardner, J. W. (1990). <u>On leadership.</u> New York: Free Press.

Gilligan, C. (1982, 1993). <u>In a different voice, psychological theory and women's development.</u> Cambridge MA: Harvard University Press

Graham, P. Ed. (1995). <u>Mary parker folley-prophet of management.</u> Boston:Harvard Business School Press.

Greenleaf, R. (1976). <u>Servant leadership.</u> New York: Paulist Press.

Grof, S. (1990). <u>The holotropic mind.</u> San Francisco, Harper.

Handy, C. (1992). Balancing corporate power: A new federalist paper. <u>Harvard Business Review</u>(November-December), 59-72.

Hawken, P. (1993). <u>The ecology of commerce</u>. San Francisco: HarperBusiness

Hegel, G. (1997). <u>Phenomenology of spirit.</u> San Francisco, Jossey Bass:

Heifetz. R.A., (1994). <u>Leadership without easy answers.</u> President and Fellows of Harvard College.

Henrickson, R. L. (1989). <u>Leadership and culture.</u> Unpublished doctoral dissertation, University of San Diego, San Diego, CA.

James, W. (1929). <u>Th varieties of religious experience.</u> New York: The Modern Library.

Jaworski, J., (1996). <u>Synchronicity, the inner path of leadership.</u> San Francisco Berrett-Kowgler

Jung C. (1964). <u>Man and his symbols.</u> New York: Aldus Books

King. U. (1994). Spirituality for life. In Mananzan, M., Oduyoye, M., Tanez, E., Clarkson, J., Grey, M., and Russel, L, (Ed). <u>Women resisting violence, spirituality for life.</u> (pp. 147-160). Morknoll, NY: Orbis Books.

Klein, E., & Izzo, J. B. (1997). Awakening corporate soul, four paths to unleash the power of people at work. Canada: Fairwinds Books.

Luke, H. (1995). The way of women, awakening the perennial feminine. New York: Doubleday.

Matthews, C, (1992). Sophia, goddess of wisdom the divine feminine from black goddess to world soul. Great Britain, The Bath Press.

Mandela, N. (1994). Long walk to freedom, the autobiography of nelson mandela. Boston: Little, Brown & Company.

Maslow, A. H. (1970). Motivation and personality. (2nd ed.) New York Harper & Row, Publishers.

Kouzes, J.M., & Pozner, B.Z. (1995). The leadership challenge. San Francisco: Jossey-Bass Inc.

Marcic, D. (1997). Managing with the wisdom of love, uncovering virtue in people and organizations. San Francisco: Jossey-Bass Inc.

Mello, J. A. (1998). Reframing leadership pedagogy through model and theory building, Article in Leadership in Management.

Morgan, (1986). The postmodern organization. New York: Simon & Schuster Inc.

Machiovelli, N. (1532, 1986), The prince. New York: Prometheus Books.

O'Brien, W. J. (1998). The soul of corporate leadership, guidelines for values-centered governance. In Innovations in Management Series., Waltham: Pegasus Communications, Inc.

Palmer, P. J. (1994). Leading from within. Conger, J. Ed. Spirit at work. San Francisco: Jossey-Bass.

Peck, S.M. (1986). The road less traveled. New York: Simon & Schuster Inc.

Peck, S.M. (1987). The different drum, community making and peace. New York: Simon & Schuster Inc.

Pienta, D. A. (1987). A values hierarchy. In S. M. Natale (2nd Ed.), Ethics and morals in business. Birmingham: REP.

Putnam, R. (1995). Bowling alone, america's declining social capital. Journal of Democracy, January p. 65-78.

Roberts, J.M., (1993), History of the world. New York: Oxford University Pdfress.

Rost, J. C. (1991). Leadership for the 21st century. Westport: Praeger.

Rost, J. C. (1993). Leadership and shared governance. Presented at the Shared Governce: Seazing the Opportunity for Educational Leadership Workshop for Community College Administrators.

Schein, E. H. (1992). Organizational Culture and Leadership. (2nd ed.). San Francisco: Jossey-Bass.

Schwartz, T. (1995). What really matters, searching for wisdom in america. New York: Bantam books.

Senge, P. M. (1990). The fifth discipline. New York: Doubleday/Currency.

Smart, B. (1990). Modernity, postmodernity and the present. In B.S. Turner (Ed.), Theories of modernity and postmodernity (pp. 14-30). London: Sage.

Smith, H. (1991). The world's religions: Our great wisdom traditions. San Francisco: Harper San Francisco.

Spretnak, C. (1982, 1994). The politics of women's spirituality. New York: Doubleday.

Teilhard de Chardin P. (1944, 1965). The phenomenon of man. New York: Harper & Row.

Toffler, A. & Toffler, H. (1994, 1995). Creating a new civilization, the politics of the third wave. Atlanta GA: Turner Publishing, Inc.

Wade, J. (1996). Changes of mind, a holonomic theory of the evolution of consciousness. New York: State University of New York Press.

Wheatley, M. J. (1994). Leadership and the new science. San Franciso, Berett-Koehler.

Wilber, K. (1996). A brief history of everything. Boston: Shambhala.

Wilber, K. (1980, 1983, 1990). Eye to eye, the quest for the new paradigm, (3rd Ed). Boston: Shambhala.

Wilber, K. (1997). The eye of spirit, an integral vision for a world gone slightly mad. Boston: Shambhala.

Whyte, D. (1994). The heart aroused, poetry and the preservation of the soul in corporate america. New York: Currency Doublday.

Zullo, J. R., (1996, October). <u>Leadership and adult development: postindustrial paradigms and parallels.</u> Paper presented at the Leadership conference at the University of San Diego, San Diego, CA.

ABOUT THE AUTHOR

Lisa Aldon is a leadership development consultant and founder of *Transcendent Leadership (www.transcendentleadership.com)*. She has her Master's degree in Leadership Studies from the University of San Diego with a concentration in organizational change and a Bachelor of Science in Mechanical Engineering Technology with a minor in Solar Energy from Arizona State University. Most of her 20-year career has been in the engineering manufacturing industry, with the last 10 years serving as a manager and team leader. Lisa also worked at the Nizhoni School for Global Consciousness where she also taught high school science, math and leadership to our "higher consciousness" global youth.

LaVergne, TN USA
15 October 2010
200856LV00003B/100/A